CW00922759

"Matt McCullough's meditation on death is haunting, profound, and stirring, reminding us of our identity and our destiny apart from Jesus Christ. Death casts a shadow over our lives, showing us, as McCullough points out, that we aren't the center of the universe. Those who live rightly and those who live forever often think of death, but at the same time they live with hope since Jesus is the resurrection and the life. This book reminds us why we die and teaches us how to live."

Thomas R. Schreiner, James Buchanan Harrison Professor of New Testament Interpretation, The Southern Baptist Theological Seminary

"This is a brilliant book. Rightly advocating 'death awareness' but not 'death acceptance,' McCullough powerfully demonstrates that in order to remember Christ well, we need to learn to remember death well. This book shines with scriptural truth, pouring forth the light of Christ upon our fleeting, fear-filled lives."

Matthew Levering, James N. and Mary D. Perry, Jr. Chair of Theology, Mundelein Seminary; author, *Dying and the Virtues*

"This is a profoundly helpful book. With a preacher's turn of phrase and illustrative eye, with a pastor's care for precious people and their greatest fears, and with a theologian's grasp of the Bible's big picture and the heart of the gospel, Matthew McCullough writes to overcome our detachment from death and deepen our attachment to the Lord Jesus Christ. These pages will repay careful thought and meditative reflection on their surprising riches."

David Gibson, Minister, Trinity Church, Aberdeen, Scotland; author, *Living Life Backward*; coeditor, *From Heaven He Came and Sought Her*

"Can we face death and find hope? According to Matt McCullough, yes. *Remember Death* rightly reorients us to the impermanence of this world and the brevity of our lives, witnessing to the paradox that grief is necessary for faith. Richly informed by Scripture and a feast of other sources, this book vitally forms our longings for the world to come. I can't wait to recommend it."

Jen Pollock Michel, author, *Teach Us to Want* and *Keeping Place*

"Through the lens of Scripture, McCullough looks death squarely in the eye and reminds us that it is nothing to be afraid of. For the Christian, it has truly lost its sting. *Remember Death* is a welcome conversation in a culture that doesn't know how to think about mortality."

Andrew Peterson, singer/songwriter; author, The Wingfeather Saga series; Founder, The Rabbit Room

Remember
Death

Other Gospel Coalition Books

15 Things Seminary Couldn't Teach Me, edited by Collin Hansen and Jeff Robinson Sr.

Coming Home: Essays on the New Heaven and New Earth, edited by D. A. Carson and Jeff Robinson Sr.

Don't Call It a Comeback: The Old Faith for a New Day, edited by Kevin DeYoung

Entrusted with the Gospel: Pastoral Expositions of 2 Timothy, edited by D. A. Carson

Glory in the Ordinary: Why Your Work in the Home Matters to God, by Courtney Reissig

God's Love Compels Us: Taking the Gospel to the World, edited by D. A. Carson and Kathleen B. Nielson

God's Word, Our Story: Learning from the Book of Nehemiah, edited by D. A. Carson and Kathleen B. Nielson

The Gospel as Center: Renewing Our Faith and Reforming Our Ministry Practices, edited by D. A. Carson and Timothy Keller

Gospel-Centered Youth Ministry: A Practical Guide, edited by Cameron Cole and Jon Nielson

Here Is Our God: God's Revelation of Himself in Scripture, edited by Kathleen B. Nielson and D. A. Carson

His Mission: Jesus in the Gospel of Luke, edited by D. A. Carson and Kathleen B. Nielson

The New City Catechism: 52 Questions and Answers for Our Hearts and Minds

The New City Catechism Devotional: God's Truth for Our Hearts and Minds

The Pastor as Scholar and the Scholar as Pastor: Reflections on Life and Ministry, by John Piper and D. A. Carson, edited by David Mathis and Owen Strachan

Praying Together: The Priority and Privilege of Prayer: In Our Homes, Communities, and Churches, by Megan Hill

Pursuing Health in an Anxious Age, by Bob Cutillo

Remember Death: The Surprising Path to Living Hope, by Matthew McCullough

The Scriptures Testify about Me: Jesus and the Gospel in the Old Testament, edited by D. A. Carson

Seasons of Waiting: Walking by Faith When Dreams Are Delayed, by Betsy Childs Howard

Word-Filled Women's Ministry: Loving and Serving the Church, edited by Gloria Furman and Kathleen B. Nielson

Remember Death

The Surprising Path to Living Hope

Matthew McCullough

Foreword by Russell Moore

WHEATON, ILLINOIS

Hardcover ISBN: 978-1-4335-6053-8
ePub ISBN: 978-1-4335-6056-9
PDF ISBN: 978-1-4335-6054-5
Mobipocket ISBN: 978-1-4335-6055-2

Library of Congress Cataloging-in-Publication Data

Names: McCullough, Matthew, author.
Title: Remember death : the surprising path to living hope / Matthew McCullough.
Description: Wheaton : Crossway, 2018. | Includes bibliographical references and index.
Identifiers: LCCN 2017035953 (print) | LCCN 2018025011 (ebook) | ISBN 9781433560545 (pdf) | ISBN 9781433560552 (mobi) | ISBN 9781433560569 (epub) | ISBN 9781433560538 (hc)
Subjects: LCSH: Death—Religious aspects—Christianity.
Classification: LCC BT825 (ebook) | LCC BT825 .M353 2018 (print) | DDC 236/.1—dc23
LC record available at https://lccn.loc.gov/2017035953

Crossway is a publishing ministry of Good News Publishers.

LB		29	28	27	26	25	24	23	22	21	20	19
14	13	12	11	10	9	8	7	6	5	4	3	2

For my sons,
Walter, Sam, and Benjamin

———

Let this be recorded for a generation to come,
so that a people yet to be created may praise the Lord:
that he looked down from his holy height;
from heaven the Lord looked at the earth,
to hear the groans of the prisoners,
to set free those who were doomed to die,
that they may declare in Zion the name of the Lord,
and in Jerusalem his praise,
when peoples gather together,
and kingdoms, to worship the Lord.

Psalm 102:18–22

Contents

Foreword

by Russell Moore

Years ago I was driving through a rural area of west Tennessee, on my way to a little cottage on the Pickwick Dam in north Mississippi, where I would take a couple of days away to write. Much was on my mind. I had large decisions in front of me—decisions that would shape the whole course of my future. My immediate problem was not the course of my future, but the course of my actual journey at the time. I was lost. Every turn I took seemed to get me farther out into the woods and farther away from any recognizable landmark. This was before the advent of global positioning technology, and even if it were now, such technology would have done me little good, since my phone could not access a signal. I turned into the first driveway I saw to tinker with my phone long enough to get a cell signal to call someone who might give me directions. It took a moment or two for me to realize that I was in a church graveyard, and my phone was still the deadest thing there.

Sometimes, not often enough, I feel a strong prompting to stop everything and pray. Sometimes, far too often, I ignore that prompting, and conclude that I'm too busy to stop. This time I had no choice but to stop. I had nowhere to go. I stopped and walked around that graveyard, and churchyard, praying for God to grant me some wisdom and discernment about the large life decision I had in front of me. As I wandered in front of the little Baptist church building, I was still praying, but my eyes were lazily scanning the red brick in front of me. I stopped as I read the cornerstone, engraved sometime in the years before I was born. The date was there, and right beneath it: "Herman Russell Moore, pastor." I stopped praying, startled. Herman Russell Moore was the name of my paternal grandfather, who died when I was five years old. And my grandfather was a pastor, serving many churches in Mississippi and Tennessee. When my phone finally had cell service, my first call was not to my office, but to my grandmother. I gave her the name of the church and asked if she'd ever heard of it. "Of course," she said. "Your grandfather was pastor there."

I was stunned speechless, and just kept repeating to myself, "What are the odds?" But I did not want to waste the sign, whatever it was that in God's providence had directed me there. So I kept praying, walking around the graves. I wondered about the people there, in the ground beneath me. How many of them had heard my grandfather preach the gospel? How many found Jesus in the church behind me? How many had prayed with my grandfather to receive Christ, or at the funeral of a loved one, or maybe even, like I was then, as they were facing a major life decision. They were gone now.

But I then thought about who in the ground beneath me might have been a thorn in the flesh to my grandfather. How many had criticized his preaching or questioned whether he did hospital visits often enough? Maybe someone had even, as is sadly all-too-regular practice in some churches, started an anonymous letter campaign to oppose the building of that sanctuary. They were gone too.

In that moment, I came to realize that maybe, as Tolkien put it, "not all who wander are lost." Perhaps I was there for just this reason, to contemplate that whatever it was that had filled my grandfather with joy during his time here, and whatever had kept him up worrying at night, much of it was buried beneath me. The building, where the gospel was, I presumed, still preached, was still there. But even that would not be permanent, but would one day be swept aside by time, replaced by—who knows?—a restaurant chain or a Buddhist meditation clinic. All of that would also be swept away in the trillions of years of cosmic time stretching out ahead of us.

The decision I was mulling seemed so important to me at the moment. It seemed to be of existential importance. And yet, as I stood on cemetery grounds, I was reminded that I would die. I, like this church, and like my ancestor who served it, would pass away as a vapor (James 4:14), as a forgotten stalk of grass (Ps. 103:15–16). My decision seemed, on the one hand, even more important. After all, my grandfather's ministry here was part of a chain of decisions, without which I would not even exist to contemplate that place. On the other hand, my decision seemed much less important. I was reminded, despite the fact that I was, at the time, a young man in the whirl of the prime of my career, that I was just a dying creature, who would one day be forgotten, along with all my big plans and my fears and anxieties. At that moment, the thought of my mortality did not leave me with a sense of futility or dread. The thought was strangely liberating, freeing me, if just for a second, to reflect on what really matters—to give thanks to God for giving me a gospel to believe and people to love.

That's what I pray this book does for you. I pray that you come away from a book on mortality with a sense of clarity about what really matters—about *who* really matters. I pray that this book, as it leads you to reflect on your own coming demise, gives you a sense of joy, of gratitude, of longing to be part of that great cloud of witnesses in heaven. I pray that this book is useful to you, but

I pray more that this book turns out to be a waste of your time. I pray that you and I don't ever actually succumb to death, but that, instead, we are part of the generation that sees the eastern skies explode with the glory of the returning King of Israel, the Lord Jesus Christ. But, even if so, the lessons of this book will be worth your time, to call you away from seeing yourself as a messiah or as a devil, as a Caesar or as a Judas. Your life is worth living, precisely because it is not your life at all. Your life—at least in this moral frame—has a beginning and an end. But your life—your real life—is hidden with Christ (Col. 3:3). That then gives you the freedom to lose your life in sacrifice to others, in obedience to God, in order to save it.

I wish that I could say that my accidental visit to that church graveyard permanently changed my life. I wish I could write that I don't still grapple with an illusion of immortality or with worry about tomorrow. I can't say that. What I can say, though, is that sometimes God will let us get a little bit lost, so that we might look about and realize that we are not phoenixes rising from our own ashes but we are sheep, following the voice of a shepherd, even through the valley of the shadow of death. Maybe such a moment of clarity will come for you as you find yourself lost in the truths of this book. If so, you might realize that you are not as lost as you think, but that you are instead being led through the graveyard of your own fallen life, onward toward home.

Acknowledgments

I want to speak first to my fellow members at Trinity Church. There really is no other place to begin. Anything useful in this book flows out of our life together. Thank you, friends, for opening your lives to me. For working with me to see the relevance of Jesus to what you're facing. For being so patient with me as I've learned how to teach you the Bible. And for putting up with, arguably, more than your share of sermons on death and resurrection.

I owe a special thanks to the elders and staff who have shouldered the burden of leadership with me and given me the space to work on this book: Matt Givens, Lane Hamilton, Will Harvey, Bill Heerman, Dave Hunt, Seth Jones, Laura Magness, Shaka Mitchell, Justin Myers, Drew Raines, and Jason Tan. Thank you for giving me the joy of serving our church with you.

Collin Hansen is the reason this book has reached the light of day. For some reason he took interest when I barely had an idea. He's guided me step by step through uncharted territory ever since. Thank you, brother, for sharing wisdom, grace, and friendship with me. And for introducing me to Justin Taylor and the wonderful team at Crossway. It's been an honor to work with a publisher whose books have been such a blessing to me over the years.

I wrote most of a first draft on a sabbatical with my family at Tyndale House in Cambridge. That place is otherworldly, in a good way. Thank you to Peter Williams, the staff, and the fellows who made my time there so fruitful and enjoyable.

We couldn't have made the trip to Cambridge without the hospitality of Bobby and Kristin Jamieson, who gave us the use of their home while we were there. As if that weren't enough, Bobby was the first to read a rough draft, and his careful suggestions made a huge difference.

Besides Collin and Bobby, several other friends offered well-timed advice on the manuscript at one stage or another. I'm especially grateful to Drew D'Agostino, Jonathan Leeman, Drew Raines (again), Amy Tan, and Adrian Taylor. All of you sharpened the final product and, in more than a couple places, saved me from myself.

My father, Mark, also offered precious feedback in the early stages. But far more than that, he was the first to model the perspective at the heart of this book. Thank you, Dad, for teaching me to love the good things of life, to recognize that they're passing away, and to prioritize what lasts. No son has had a more faithful "forward scout in the wilderness of time."

I am grateful most of all to my wife and children. Lindsey, ever since we were kids, I've been amazed that God would give me such a friend. There are no words. Thank you for sharing these days under the sun with me. And for doing more than anyone else to prepare me for the endless day to come. I love you.

Walter, Sam, and Benjamin, you have brought unimaginable joy to our lives. Watching you grow has done more than anything to break my heart over the passing of time, and to make me long for when all things are only and always new. I wrote this book thinking of you guys. It's dedicated to you, with the prayer I will offer as long as I live: that you will hold fast to the only comfort in life and in death, Christ in you, the hope of glory.

Introduction

I don't know of anyone who survived more near-death experiences than WWII airman Louis Zamperini. After volunteering for the Army Air Forces, Zamperini survived months of flight training when thousands of others did not. He survived bombing missions under heavy fire, one of which left nearly six hundred bullet holes in the fuselage of his B-24. After mechanical failure sent his plane plunging into the Pacific Ocean, he survived the crash. And that's when his survival story really began.

He lived for weeks on a small inflatable raft, baked by the sun and tossed by violent storms. He had nothing to drink but whatever rainwater he could collect. He had nothing to eat but the fish and birds he caught with his hands and ate raw. He fought off swarms of sharks that constantly followed his raft and often lunged to pull him in. He dodged the bullets of a Japanese plane he had hoped would be his rescuer.

Zamperini spent forty-seven days on this raft, longer than anyone else had ever survived adrift at sea. Then, when he finally reached land, he was captured immediately. He spent the next two years as a prisoner of war, transferred from one horrific camp to another, suffering relentlessly under forced labor, starvation, disease, and merciless torture. When his camp was finally liberated, he was skin and bones, barely clinging to life. More than one in three of his fellow American prisoners had died. Yet still, somehow, he survived.[1]

It isn't difficult to see why Zamperini's biography, *Unbroken*, has sold millions of copies. It is a captivating story very well told. And in a way, it makes sense that the book's subtitle calls it a "story of survival." It is. Or, rather, it was.

Nearly seventy years after his return from war, Zamperini faced what his family called the greatest challenge of his life—a forty-day battle with pneumonia. According to those who stood beside him, "his indomitable courage and fighting spirit were never more apparent." But at ninety-seven years old, his body was a far cry from the specimen that competed in the 1936 Olympic Games. Worn down by time, the man who fought off starvation and shark attacks and deadly dysentery and sadistic prison guards finally entered a battle he could not survive. On July 2, 2014, Louis Zamperini died.[2]

Lauren Hillenbrand's account of Zamperini's life works as a survival story because the book concludes in 2008. At one level, calling Zamperini's or anyone else's story a survival story is like describing a fall from a thirty-story building a survival story because it ends before the subject hits the ground.

Perhaps my point is a little cliché, but I hope at least it's clear: it may not be the fall that kills you, but something always does. No one gets out of life alive. Zoomed out a bit more, there's no such thing as a survival story.

Still, I wonder: when is the last time you thought of the fact that you will die? When did you last have a conversation with someone on the subject of death? Have you ever seen anyone

---

1. Laura Hillenbrand, *Unbroken: A World War II Story of Survival, Resilience, and Redemption* (New York: Random House, 2010).

2. For these details, see the obituary published by Aleksandra Gjorgievska, "Olympian and World War II Hero Louis Zamperini Dies at 97," *Time*, July 3, 2014, http://time.com/2953878/louis-zamperini-obituary/.

die? Ever had someone die in your home? When did you last walk through a cemetery or attend a funeral? Have you read any book, watched any movie, even listened to any sermon that deals with the problem of death? I'm not talking about death by violence or death by accident or death by rare and virulent disease. I'm talking about death as a basic human experience—as basic as birth, eating, and sleeping.

Death is a fundamental human experience, uniting all humans across time and space, race and class. But in our time and place, death isn't something we think about very often, if at all. In chapter 1 I'll get into the reasons for this avoidance—both how we're able to avoid the subject and why we'd want to. But, in short, the remarkable achievements of modern medicine have pushed death further and further back in the average Western person's life span. We enjoy better disease prevention, better pharmaceutical treatments, and better emergency care than any other society in history. That's a wonderful blessing, no question. But it comes with a major side effect: many of us can afford to live most of our lives as if death isn't our problem.

Death is no less inevitable than it's ever been, but many of us don't have to see it or even think about it as a daily presence in our lives. When people die, it is more likely than not in a medical facility, cordoned off from where we live, a sanitized, carefully managed, even industrial process that occurs when professionals decide to stop giving care. Death is still inevitable, but it has become bizarre.

Death has also become a taboo of sorts, not to be discussed in polite company. We label such talk as "morbid." It's a pejorative term applied to words or ideas that are unusually dark—distortions of the truth as we wish to see it. To bring up the subject of death is too often awkward at best, shameful at worst.

But try as we might to avoid the subject, every one of us experiences death's shadow every day. It shows up in our insecurities about who we are and why we matter. It shows up in our dissatisfaction with the things we believe should make us happy. And it shows up in our pain over the loss of every good thing that doesn't last long enough. We can't avoid death and its effects. We shouldn't avoid talking about it either.

Our detachment from death puts us out of line with the perspective of the Bible. Throughout its pages, whether law or history or poetry or prophecy or gospel or letter, death is a fixation far more common than in our lives today. For biblical authors an awareness of death and its implications for life is crucial for a life of wisdom.

Consider, for example, the prayer of Psalm 90: "Teach us to number our days that we may get a heart of wisdom" (v. 12). That's a euphemistic way of saying "teach us to recognize our death." The prayer comes as a sort of hinge between the two parts of the psalm. The first part focuses on human limitations compared with the vastness of God. For God time is nothing. "From everlasting to everlasting you are God" (90:2). "For a thousand years in your sight are but as yesterday when it is past, or as a watch in the night" (90:4). But for us humans, under sin and judgment, time destroys everything. Our lives are "like a dream." Our lives are like the grass: "in the morning it flourishes and is renewed; in the evening it fades and withers" (90:5–6). At best, "the years of our life are seventy, or even by reason of strength eighty; yet their span is but toil and trouble; they are soon gone, and we fly away" (90:10). The psalmist's prayer for remembrance of death is a prayer for a life of humility, a perspective that understands our limits and the insurmountable difference between God and us.

But this prayer sets up another theme in the second part of the psalm. Immediately after praying that God would teach us to number our days, the psalmist prays that God would make us glad all our days with the richness of his love: "Satisfy us in the morning with your steadfast love, that we may rejoice and be glad all our days" (Ps. 90:14).

I believe those two prayers go hand in hand: teach me to live with the reality of my death so that I can live in the gladness of your love. Before I can be astounded by God's love—before I will see the beauty of his love more clearly than the problems of my life—I must see my desperate need of it and my thorough unworthiness of it. When God teaches us to number our days, he protects us from prideful self-deception and enables us to live with genuine, realistic gladness.

This is a book about death because wisdom comes from honesty about the world as it is. I want to help us number our days—to remember death—as a form of spiritual discipline. I want to show from the Bible the illuminating power of death-awareness for the lives we're living now.[3]

I am not writing primarily to those facing imminent death or to those grieving the loss of a loved one, though I hope my observations would encourage them.[4] I'm writing to convince those living like immortals that they're not actually immortal—to help

---

3. I will often use "death-awareness" as a shorthand description of the perspective I advocate in this book. I first noticed the term in Julian Barnes, *Nothing to Be Frightened Of* (New York: Vintage, 2008).

4. There is a branch of Christian tradition known as the *ars moriendi*—the "art of dying." In the ancient church, teaching on how to achieve a good death was common, and manuals on best practices offered formulas that shaped the deaths of the faithful for centuries. For background information, see Philippe Aries, *Western Attitudes toward Death: From the Middle Ages to the Present*, trans. Patricia Ranum (Baltimore: Johns Hopkins University Press, 1974). For a contemporary book offering advice on preparing well for death, see Rob Moll, *The Art of Dying: Living Fully into the Life to Come* (Downers Grove, IL: InterVarsity, 2010). For personal memoirs on facing death as a Christian, see Todd Billings, *Rejoicing in Lament: Wrestling with Incurable Cancer and Life in Christ* (Grand Rapids, MI: Brazos, 2015); Russ Ramsey, *Struck: One Christian's Reflections on Encountering Death* (Downers Grove, IL: InterVarsity, 2017). For recent helpful books on how to grieve in hope, see Timothy Keller, *Walking with God through Pain and Suffering* (New York: Dutton, 2013); Christopher Ash, *Job: The Wisdom of the Cross* (Wheaton, IL: Crossway, 2014). For modern classics see these works by C. S. Lewis: *The Problem of Pain: How Human Suffering Raises Almost Intolerable Intellectual Problems* (New York: Macmillan, 1962); *A Grief Observed* (New York: Bantam, 1976).

them gain the realistic perspective that the grieving or terminally ill already have.[5]

I'm writing to those for whom death feels remote and unreal—something that happens to other people—to help them see how a present acquaintance with death is important for the lives they're living now.

This purpose places my book within a stream of time-honored Christian reflection called *memento mori*. Roughly translated, it's the title for this book: remember death. The focus of this tradition is on recognizing death—thinking about what it means for us and where we experience its effects—in order to live a true, faithful, joyful life in the meantime.

I was first struck by this practice in graduate school, training as a church historian, when for a time I studied the ministries of the Puritans in England and America.[6] It was difficult to miss the disjunction. What was central to them is mostly absent from Western culture now, and from my experience of American Christianity.

Then in my first years as a pastor, preaching verse by verse through books of the Bible, I came to recognize in a new way just how often the Bible speaks of death. I knew of its focus on the

---

5. In other words, this is not a book about how to die well, though reflection on facing the end of life in faith is a wonderful part of the Christian tradition. Nor is this a book on how to grieve the loss of a loved one, though I pray it will offer useful perspective for those who want to mourn in hope. These two branches of reflection—how to die in faith and how to grieve in hope—are crucial for all of us who believe. They address experiences all of us will share. These books must be written. I'm just not the man to write one of them.

Full disclosure: I am in the first years of my life as a pastor. I pastor a church of mostly young people who are preparing for lives that are mostly in front of them. I've had my share of opportunities to help my friends face suffering with the promises of the gospel. But I have not guided anyone through the final days of life. And I haven't preached a funeral service for a member who has died. I expect those days are coming. But I don't yet have the experience to write a book full of practical advice on how to face death as a Christian.

6. There is a good example of this emphasis in Richard Baxter's influential guide to pastoral ministry, *The Reformed Pastor* (1656; repr., Carlisle, PA: Banner of Truth, 1974). "O sirs, surely if you had all conversed with neighbor Death as oft as I have done, and as often received the sentence in yourselves, you would have an unquiet conscience, if not a reformed life, as to your ministerial diligence and fidelity" (204).

problem of sin and the problem of eternal judgment. What struck me was its focus on physical death—the fact that our lives in this world come to an end. The problem of death is surely connected to the problem of sin and the problem of judgment, as part of the effects of human rebellion on this broken world. But death is an aspect of the human condition worthy of its own attention, especially in a culture that wants to deny its grip.

All that said, this isn't really a book about death. It's a book about Jesus and, therefore, a book about hope. I have come to see, as the pastor of young up-and-comers, how important death-awareness can be for confronting a problem I believe goes hand in hand with the avoidance of death. When the reality of death is far from our minds, the promises of Jesus often seem detached from our lives. These promises seem abstract, belonging to another world from the one I'm living in, disconnected from the problems that dominate my field of view.

Contrast that to what Peter says about the relevance of Jesus in 1 Peter 1. Peter describes Christians as those who are "born again to a living hope through the resurrection of Jesus Christ from the dead" (1 Pet. 1:3). Peter assumes that the resurrection of Jesus means *living hope* for those who trust in him. This hope is not distant or otherworldly but broadcast in and for this life. But look at what he says about the object of that hope: "an inheritance that is imperishable, undefiled, and unfading, kept in heaven for you" (1:4).

Perhaps your eyes glaze over when you read words like that. Perhaps these words even stir some anger. Imperishable? Undefiled? Unfading? Why should I care? I don't need an inheritance kept in heaven. I need help now, in this world. Perhaps you feel this way about many of Jesus's promises. What good is blood sacrifice or justification when you're facing an uncertain job market or worried you'll never find a spouse? How can

I care about an immortal body when I'm ashamed of the one I have now? And why does Jesus talk so much about eternal life? I don't just need a path to glory land. I need to know how to cope with hard things today.

If you feel this way about the promises of Jesus, I believe it is because you don't think nearly enough about death. Consider the way Peter wraps up his great chapter on hope. At the end of the first chapter, returning again to language like "born again" and "imperishable," Peter quotes from Isaiah 40:

> "All flesh is like grass
>> and all its glory like the flower of grass.
> The grass withers,
>> and the flower falls,
> but the word of the Lord remains forever."
>
> And this word is the good news that was preached to you. (1 Pet. 1:24–25)

Do you see what Peter is doing? To bring the imperishable hope his readers have in Christ down to earth, into their everyday, he's pointing them to why they need it so badly. Imperishable. Undefiled. Unfading. These are relative terms. They are defined by what they're not. They only make sense when compared with what they negate. Perishable. Defiled. Fading. That's why Peter ends the chapter with a reminder that everything around them is perishing, like newly sprouted grass in the dry summer heat. Nothing lasts, good or bad. Except for one thing: the Word of the Lord. The gospel preached to you. Jesus Christ crucified and resurrected.

Before you long for a life that is imperishable, you must accept that you are perishing along with everyone you care about. You must recognize that anything you might accomplish or acquire in this world is already fading away. Only then will you crave the unfading glory of what Jesus has accomplished and acquired for you. And you need to recognize you are going to lose everything you love in this world before you will hope in an inheritance kept in heaven for you.

Even if your life plays out in precisely the way you imagine for yourself in your wildest dreams, death will steal away everything you have and destroy everything you accomplish. As long as we're consumed by the quest for more out of this life, Jesus's promises will always seem otherworldly to us. He doesn't offer more of what death will only steal from us in the end. He offers us righteousness, adoption, God-honoring purpose, eternal life—things that taste sweet to us only when death is a regular companion.

If we want to see the beauty of Jesus, we must first look carefully and honestly at death. I appreciate the way Walter Wangerin captured this connection in a wonderful book on death and joy written more than twenty-five years ago:

> If the gospel seems irrelevant to our daily lives, that is our fault, not the gospel's. For if death is not a daily reality, then Christ's triumph over death is neither daily nor real. Worship and proclamation and even faith itself take on a dream-like, unreal air, and Jesus is reduced to something like a long-term insurance policy, filed and forgotten—whereas he can be our necessary ally, an immediate, continuing friend, the holy destroyer of death and the devil, my own beautiful savior.[7]

By avoiding the truth about death, we're avoiding the truth about Jesus. Jesus didn't promise us so many of the things we want most out of life. He promised us victory over death. So we must learn to see the shadow of death behind the problems of life before we can recognize the powerful relevance of Jesus to every

---

7. Walter Wangerin, *Mourning into Dancing* (Grand Rapids, MI: Zondervan, 1992), 29–30.

obstacle we face. This is a book about death because it is a book about Jesus.

There's one more layer to my subject. As hope comes alive, as it spreads through the ins and outs and twists and turns of your life, the fruit that it bears is joy—joy that's resilient and realistic, that doesn't have to sweep the hard things under the rug in order to survive (1 Pet. 1:6–8). The ironic claim at the heart of this book is that the best way to enjoy your life is to get honest about your death.

When the reality of death fades to the background of our consciousness, other joy-stealing problems are quick to rise up and fill the void. French philosopher Blaise Pascal put his finger on this problem four hundred years ago. He noticed the way most people seemed indifferent to "the loss of their being" but intensely concerned about everything else: "They fear the most trifling things, foresee and feel them; and the same man who spends so many days and nights in fury and despair at losing some office or at some imaginary affront to his honor is the very one who knows that he is going to lose everything through death but feels neither anxiety nor emotion. It is a monstrous thing to see one and the same heart at once so sensitive to minor things and so strangely insensitive to the greatest."[8]

Pascal's insight is perhaps even more important today: when death is pushed out of our thinking, it isn't replaced by warmth and peace and happiness. It is replaced by others of death's many faces. We fixate instead on the comparatively trivial symptoms of our deeper problem. We are still anxious, still defensive, still insecure, still angry and even despairing. We detach ourselves from death so we can focus our time and energy on pursuing happiness. But that detachment hasn't changed the fact of our mortality, and it hasn't ultimately made us happier.

---

8. Blaise Pascal, *Pensées*, trans. A. J. Krailsheimer (New York: Penguin, 1966), 159.

To know Jesus should be to know joy. Yet isn't it true that our joy in life is often checked by pride, fear, envy, futility, dissatisfaction, and a host of other cares? I argue that an honest awareness of death puts these enemies of joy in their proper place, so that in turn the victory of Jesus can shine in its proper light. In other words, if we want to live with resilient joy—a joy that's tethered not to shifting circumstances but to the rock-solid accomplishments of Jesus—we must look honestly at the problem of death. That may be ironic, but it's biblical, and it's true.

The Plan of the Book

If we are to channel death-awareness into deeper love for the promises of the gospel, many of us must first grow reacquainted with the problem of death. We need to consider what sort of problem death is, and we need to learn how to recognize its shadow in places we may not have noticed before. Once we've learned to see the shadow, we'll be able to apply the light of Christ.

This is why I've chosen to treat the problem of death on its own, apart from the Bible's teaching about eternal judgment after death. Given what the Bible says about hell, the end of our lives in this world is almost nothing compared with the prospect of an eternal, tormented separation from God. But the problem of death has its own devastating effects on our present lives. It's a problem to which we've paid far too little attention. And it's a problem that shows up in the lives of all people, Christian or not. My hope is to describe this problem in a way that's recognizable for you no matter your religious background, so that whether you believe or not, you want the message of Jesus to be true.

In each of chapters 2–4, I begin with one of three major dimensions of death and explain where it shows up in our experience.

Then in each chapter I pair that dimension of death with the promises of Jesus that shine brighter against its dark backdrop.

In chapter 2 I discuss death and the problem of identity—what death says about who we are. By nature, we can't imagine the world without us in it. That's partly because we carry a built-in narcissism. We see ourselves as the lead characters in the story of the world, and everything else is defined by how it relates to us. But it's also because we rightly perceive that human lives have dignity that other animals don't have. Every person has a unique, irreplaceable identity that is precious and worthwhile. But death confronts our notions of human significance head-on.

Death makes a statement about who we are: we are not too important to die. We will die, like all those who've gone before us, and the world will keep on moving just as it always has. No one is indispensable. It's a harsh, even terrifying statement.

When we've allowed this statement to land on us and sink in, we're prepared for awe at the message of the gospel. It's another statement of identity. If death tells us we're not too important to die, the gospel tells us we're so important that Christ died for us. And not because death's message about us is wrong. It isn't. On our own, we are dispensable. But joined to Christ, through our union with him, we are righteous, we are children of God, and God will not let us die any more than he left Jesus in the grave.

In chapter 3 I focus on death and the problem of futility—what death does to anything we accomplish. We look for happiness and purpose in the next pleasurable experience, in the money and possessions we try to pile up, and in what we build for ourselves through our work. But have you ever felt satisfied with your life? Like you've done enough?

Futility is something we'll continue to feel because underneath our drive to pleasure, wealth, and success is a drive to overcome the reality of death. These things will never bear that weight.

But what if Christ has taken on death for us? What if, in fact, he is raised, in triumph over our last enemy? Then what we do with our lives, though futile as a defense against death, is not in vain after all. When we don't have to defeat death for ourselves, we're set free to enjoy what we do and to aim it at the glory of the One who has conquered for us.

In chapter 4 the subject is death and the problem of loss—what death does to everything we love. Loss isn't something that happens sometimes to unfortunate people who happened to be in the wrong place or have the wrong genetic codes. The truth is that nothing lasts, that you can never go back, and that therefore everyone loses everything to death.

How can you enjoy anything about life if you know that, in the end, the more you love something the more it will hurt when you lose it? That joy comes only if Jesus can deliver on his promise of eternal life—not an angelic, bodiless realm among the clouds, but a new world in which the things we love don't pass away. If Jesus can deliver on that promise, we're set free to enjoy the transient pleasures of this life—or to do without them—knowing they are appetizers for the endless, all-satisfying feast he has prepared for his own.

In the fifth chapter, I try to illustrate the practical effect of remembering death—how to leverage death-awareness in the fight for hopeful joy. I use several examples of common joy-stealing experiences—things like discontent, envy, and anxiety—to show how processing these things in light of death helps us process them in the light of Christ.

But first, an important step toward recovery of healthy death-awareness is deeper self-awareness. Many of us need to see how we participate in a culture that has suppressed the truth about death more than any other time and place in history.

1

Where Is Thy Sting?

Compared with most of us these days, seventeenth-century French philosopher Blaise Pascal was obsessed with death. In his *Pensées* Pascal offers one of the most disturbing images of the human condition I've ever read:

> Imagine a number of men in chains, all under sentence of death, some of whom are each day butchered in the sight of the others; those remaining see their own condition in that of their fellows, and looking at each other with grief and despair await their turn. This is an image of the human condition.[1]

That's dark, isn't it? Try for a moment to imagine yourself in Pascal's nightmare. You're one of a line of prisoners condemned to die by firing squad, one at a time. You hear the captain's call: Ready. Aim. Fire. You hear the sound of the shots. You hear a body fall to the ground. Then you hear it all over again, only this time a little closer. One by one the others before you in line are

---

1. Blaise Pascal, *Pensées*, trans. A. J. Krailsheimer (New York: Penguin, 1966), 165.

killed. And you know in every one of their deaths your own is foreshadowed. You are implicated in what is happening to them. Each death implies your own.

This is how Pascal views all of life. He is the condemned man on death row. Every death he sees around him forecasts his own. It's a sign of what will happen to him, a reminder that his turn is coming. And all he can do is wait.

Pascal lived with a sense of solidarity with the dying that is mostly unknown to many of us. Of course, we know that people die, even people close to us. But I wonder how often you see your own death foreshadowed in the death of someone else.

There are many people, of course, whose circumstances don't allow the space necessary to avoid the reality of death. Perhaps you're a physician or a hospice nurse. Perhaps you serve in the military or in law enforcement. Perhaps you belong to a majority-world nation or live in a disadvantaged community in the West, where life expectancy is lower than average.[2] You may have lost a spouse or a child. You may live even now with a terminal illness. To whatever extent you belong in a group like these, Pascal's perspective may not seem unfamiliar.

But for most people living in a modern Western context, Pascal's personal, regular engagement with death feels foreign. Perhaps Pascal's way of thinking strikes you as unstable, unhealthy, even dangerous. But before the past century Pascal's outlook was far more typical than ours. And the reality Pascal imagined hasn't changed at all. Every one of us lives with a death sentence we cannot escape. We're still waiting our turn. We're

---

2. Ta-Nehisi Coates's memoir offers a powerful example of the daily fear of violent death imposed on those who live in many African-American communities. He describes a constant awareness of his body's vulnerability, both from the sporadic and unpredictable violence of the streets and from racial bias within law enforcement. See *Between the World and Me* (New York: Spiegel and Grau, 2015).

simply less honest about the facts. Most of us no longer see what he saw.

Before we move to the problem of death and how it exposes the beauty of Jesus, we need to consider how and why so many of us have stopped paying attention to death in the first place. I want to highlight four ways we often deny death in our culture, and then ask why we're avoiding the truth.

From Home to Hospital: Where We Die Now

In 1993, a Yale surgeon and professor of medicine named Sherwin Nuland published an award-winning bestseller called *How We Die*.[3] The point of the book was to introduce unfamiliar readers to what Nuland calls "the method of modern dying"—what death typically looks like in modern-day America.[4] Each of the book's chapters takes up one of the six most common causes of death, causes like cancer and heart disease and Alzheimer's. Nuland describes the pattern of decline you can expect with each pathway and what you can do to prepare.

What is most striking to me, however, is the sheer fact that this book was necessary. In our culture, death is foreign. The book reads like a travel guide to a place you've never been. A good guide book tells you where to eat if you want to avoid the tourist traps. It tells you which sites are worth your time and money and which are overrated. It explains how to navigate transportation options, which neighborhoods have the best hotels, and how much you should expect to pay for what you'll need. You need all this from a travel guide because you haven't been to the city before. It's a stand-in for actual experience.

---

3. Sherwin Nuland, *How We Die: Reflections on Life's Final Chapter* (New York: Vintage, 1993).
4. Nuland, *How We Die*, xv.

Nuland's book is necessary because for most of us, for most of our lives, death is a foreign country. It belongs to another world. It's not just a place we've never been. It's a process we've rarely witnessed. And above all it's a reality we don't often consider. This makes our time and place different from any other time in history and most other places in the world. And Nuland's book points to the first major reason death has been shoved out of our consciousness: the incredible accomplishments of modern medicine. Over the last century medicine has made our lives longer and far more comfortable, but it has also carved out space for us to live as if we're not going to die.

A little historical context helps us see how unique our experience really is. Three hundred years ago it was impossible to avoid death, because death was everywhere. "Death dwelt within the family," as one historian put it.[5] It happened within the walls of every home. And it happened not only to your grandparents. It happened to your daddy. It happened to your little brother. It happened to your new bride. It happened to your children.

Imagine, for example, that you lived in Andover, Massachusetts, during the late 1600s. The average married couple in those years would give birth to roughly nine children. But three of the nine children would die before they were twenty-one years old. That is one of three on average. For some families the reality was far worse.[6]

Take the family of New England minister Cotton Mather, one of the most prominent citizens of his time. Mather was the father of fourteen children. Seven of his children died as infants soon after they were born. Another child died at two years old. Of the six children who survived to adulthood, five died in their twenties.

5. Gordon Geddes, *Welcome Joy: Death in Puritan New England* (Ann Arbor, MI: UMI Research Press, 1981), 57.

6. David Stannard, "Death and the Puritan Child," in David Stannard, ed., *Death in America* (Philadelphia: University of Pennsylvania Press, 1975), 18.

Only one child outlived his father. Mather enjoyed all the medical advantages available to anyone in his time. He could afford the finest care money could buy. And he buried thirteen of his children.[7]

When you got married, in other words, you expected that you would have to bury your children. When you got pregnant, you knew there was a good chance you would not survive childbirth. When your children got a fever, you weren't annoyed that they would have to miss school; you were worried they might not recover at all, and that whatever they had could mean death for everyone else in your family.[8]

The rise of modern medicine has had radical implications for the presence of death in our lives, most of them wonderful. Death in childbirth for mothers and for infants has drastically declined in the West. So has the occurrence of epidemics like smallpox or yellow fever. At the end of the eighteenth century, four out of five people died before the age of seventy. Average life expectancy was in the late thirties.[9] Now the *average* is nearly eighty years old.[10]

And we're not just living longer. We're also living better. The aches and pains earlier generations had to live with are now erased or at least covered up by new drugs, new surgical procedures, and always-developing technologies. We have drugs to attack everything from cancer cells to routine headaches. We have outpatient surgeries to relieve back pain from a herniated disk, knee pain from a torn meniscus, or cloudy vision from a cataract. These are problems our great-great-grandparents would have accepted as a normal part of life. Now doctors are remarkably good at solving them.

---

7. Stannard, "Death and the Puritan Child," 18.

8. Infectious disease was very nearly uncontrollable in the seventeenth century. During one smallpox epidemic in Boston, in 1677–1678, as many as one in every five persons died. See Stannard, "Death and the Puritan Child," 16–17.

9. Gary Laderman, *The Sacred Remains: American Attitudes toward Death, 1799–1883* (New Haven: Yale University Press, 1996), 24.

10. See, for example, "Life Expectancy," Centers for Disease Control and Prevention, http://www.cdc.gov/nchs/fastats/life-expectancy.htm, accessed August 17, 2016.

But all these medical marvels have come to us with a profound, often unnoticed side effect. The reality of death has been pushed to the margins of our experience. Every one of us still dies, but many of us don't have to think much about it.

In *Being Mortal*, surgeon Atul Gawande describes some of the effects of medicine on what he calls the "modern experience of mortality."[11] Gawande's book reflects on how medicine shapes the way we think about, confront, and ultimately experience death.

Consider, for example, that by the 1980s just 17 percent of deaths occurred in the home. In previous centuries, death happened where life happened. Death by disease was often a slow, agonizing process without the help of pain-controlling medication. This happened to someone you loved, perhaps in the room where you slept, in a place where you would see the agony and hear the moans or the screams. There was no isolating the young from the harsh reality of death. Now the experience of death has shifted from a familiar event in a familiar place—an event that occurred at the center of life—to sanitized, professionalized institutions that most people rarely visit. In the modern era, more often than not, our final days "are spent in institutions—nursing homes and intensive care units—where regimented, anonymous routines cut us off from all the things that matter to us in life."[12]

Gawande's main concern is how this relocation can be profoundly disorienting for the aged and the dying. But it has also meant a crucial shift for the young and the healthy. It is possible to live well into adulthood, even most of your life, without an up-close-and-personal encounter with death.

---

11. Atul Gawande, *Being Mortal: Medicine and What Happens in the End* (New York: Metropolitan Books, 2014), 9. Published twenty years after *How We Die*, this book confirms how accurate Nuland's insights were and how little has changed despite his warnings.

12. Gawande, *Being Mortal*, 6, 9.

Great Expectations: How We Fight Death

If modern medicine has given us the space to live as if death is not inevitable, it has also ingrained in us a powerful expectation, even a sense of entitlement, that comes to the surface when we do finally confront some life-threatening problem. In practice, patients and doctors alike behave as if death, like disease, can be eliminated. Doctors are trained to save lives— to extend life, however possible—and in the modern world they're very good at it. With this competency has grown the hope that there is always something more to be done. Some new experimental drug to try out. A new surgical procedure to perform. Another specialist to weigh in. When doctors are accustomed to winning, and when patients or their families want to grasp at every sliver of hope, it can be incredibly difficult to know when to let go.

Doctors resist letting go, in part, because the culture of their field is aimed at overcoming what isn't yet curable. Sherwin Nuland describes how over the course of his training he came to view himself as a "biomedical problem-solver." What drove him and his colleagues is what he calls "The Riddle": "The quest of every doctor in approaching serious disease is to make the diagnosis and design and carry out the specific cure. . . . The satisfaction of solving The Riddle is its own reward, and the fuel that drives the clinical engines of medicine's most highly trained specialists."[13] When The Riddle determines why and how doctors practice medicine, death will always seem like failure. Not the inevitable end of every human life, but a lost battle with some specific disease. Rather than accepting death, Nuland argues, "the most accomplished of the specialists are also the most convinced and unyielding believers in biomedicine's ability to overcome the

---

13. Nuland, *How We Die*, 248.

challenge presented by a pathological process close to claiming its victim."[14]

Patients and their families resist letting go because there is always uncertainty about how much time more treatment might provide. Gawande captures the outlook in vivid detail:

> Our every impulse is to fight, to die with chemo in our veins or a tube in our throats or fresh sutures in our flesh. The fact that we may be shortening or worsening the time we have left hardly seems to register. We imagine that we can wait until the doctors tell us that there is nothing more they can do. But rarely is there nothing more that doctors can do. They can give toxic drugs of unknown efficacy, operate to try to remove part of the tumor, put in a feeding tube if a person can't eat: there's always something.[15]

As a result of this hope in something more, "we've created a multitrillion-dollar edifice for dispensing the medical equivalent of lottery tickets—and have only the rudiments of a system to prepare patients for the near certainty that those tickets will not win." In fact, Gawande observes that in the United States Medicare devotes one quarter of its spending to "the 5 percent of patients who are in their final year of life, and most of that money goes for care in their last couple of months that is of little apparent benefit."[16]

Our approach to end-of-life care points to the cost we're paying for all the benefits we've received from medicine's ability to make life longer and more comfortable. For all that it has given us, modern medicine has enabled a powerful, pervasive self-deception. Death is no less universal now than it's ever been.

14. Nuland, *How We Die*, 265.

15. Gawande, *Being Mortal*, 173–74.

16. Gawande, *Being Mortal*, 171–72, 153. For similar stats on end-of-life care and its costs, see Ann Neumann, *The Good Death: An Exploration of Dying in America* (Boston: Beacon, 2016), 52–53.

Death is not a disease to be eliminated. It is the inevitable end of every human life. People don't die because medicine failed them. They die because they're human.

In *Swimming in a Sea of Death,* David Rieff describes the experience of his mother, writer Susan Sontag, in her struggle with cancer. This tension between the inevitability of death and the unflinching confidence in medical treatment is a major theme of Rieff's memoir. In 2004, when Sontag was diagnosed with an aggressive form of blood cancer, she threw herself into the search for a cure. Even if the available options could buy her only another year or two of life, Rieff recalls, his mother believed that in the meantime cancer research would uncover a way to buy another year or two, and so on. But, Rieff says, "it was life and not truth that she was desperate for."[17] She found doctors who were as hopeful as she was. Together they tried everything they could. But her treatment, if anything, only made matters worse. Disease and treatment worked together to strip "her both of physical dignity and mental acuity—in short, everything except her excruciating pain and her desperate hope that the course she had embarked upon would allow her to go on living."[18]

The lesson Rieff draws from this experience is a powerful check to our confidence in what medicine can do. Our success in treating a wide variety of once-fatal problems has blinded us to the fact that you have to die of something. Every time we cure one disease another will eventually rise to take its place. So many people die of cancer now because they aren't dying much earlier of influenza or smallpox or bacterial infection. If, as Rieff observes, we can "manage to turn at least many cancers into 'chronic' illnesses rather than mortal ones, what people will then

---

17. David Rieff, *Swimming in a Sea of Death: A Son's Memoir* (New York: Simon and Schuster, 2008), 102.

18. Rieff, *Swimming in a Sea of Death,* 103–4.

have to die of will be something else—something about which we will not do better, something that cannot be long remitted."[19]

Because we have conflated death and disease, we throw everything we can muster at an unsolvable problem. And in a way the harder we try to hold death off at all costs, the more ridiculous and ineffective we appear. If you've watched someone die in intensive care after being kept alive by drugs as devastating to the body as the disease itself, or tethered to life support machines for circulation of blood and oxygen, then you know what I mean. Nuland describes the intensive care unit as "a secluded treasure room of high-tech hope within the citadel in which we segregate the sick so that we may better care for them," a powerful symbol of "our society's denial of the naturalness, and even the necessity, of death."[20] If the ICU represents our all-out attempt to beat back death, it is also in a sense a monument to death's power. Here modern medicine is to death what a comb-over is to a balding scalp. We may shield the reality for a time. But at some point the comb-over is no more than a monument to the power of baldness. The harder we try, the more obvious our weakness and the more obvious death's power.

Nothing to See Here: How We Handle the Dead

Through medicine we try to avoid the inevitable. But once the inevitable has occurred, we often continue to deny the reality of death in how we treat the dead body. Many American funerary customs are profoundly unique to this time in history and this place in the world. In ways subtle and not so subtle, these customs work to blind us to the ugliness and finality of death.

In 1963 investigative journalist Jessica Mitford published *The American Way of Death*, a satirical send-up of the American

19. Rieff, *Swimming in a Sea of Death*, 167.
20. Nuland, *How We Die*, 254.

funeral industry. The book earned an unexpected spot at the top of the *New York Times* best-seller list, and for good reason. It's full of bizarre details that would be hilarious if they weren't true.

Studying trade magazines with names like *Mortuary Management*, Mitford found a startling range of products for the dead being marketed with qualities desired by the living. "The same familiar Madison Avenue language, with its peculiar adjectival range designed to anesthetize sales resistance to all sorts of products, has seeped into the funeral industry in a new and bizarre guise," Mitford wrote. "The emphasis is on the same desirable qualities that we have been schooled to look for in our daily search for excellence: comfort, durability, beauty, craftsmanship."[21]

The comfort of the deceased loved one is the primary appeal in ads for burial clothing. One company, Practical Burial Footwear of Columbus, Ohio, offered the popular and luxurious Fit-a-Fut Oxford, available in a range of leathers and either lace or goring back. Then there was the Ko-Zhee, a shoe with "soft, cushioned soles and warm, luxurious slipper comfort." What's the use of a cushioned sole for a foot that won't be walking? Their answer: "thoughtfulness and consideration for the departed."[22]

Then there are the caskets. Comfort is a major emphasis for the casket interior. You could purchase one with an adjustable soft foam mattress, for example. Or choose from a range of fabrics for the lining, from the simple softness of linen to a rich, quilted velvet. For the exterior of the casket, craftsmanship comes into play and, above all, durability. There are polished hardwoods and

---

21. Jessica Mitford, *The American Way of Death Revisited*, first Vintage ed. (1963, New York: Vintage, 2000), 15.

22. Mitford, *American Way of Death*, 34. Mitford pointed to other manufacturers that specialized in women's lingerie. Catalogs offered negligees, panties, hosiery, or, for "post mortem form restoration," the Lipari Gowns company supplied "custom burial gowns, bootees, stole, and bra." Why worry about soft undergarments no one will ever see? Presumably, once again, thoughtfulness for the departed.

brushed metals, varying in quality depending on how much you want to spend. And as of the late twentieth century, there is the expectation of a separate burial vault in which to place the casket. Why all these layers of protection? "The selling point made to the customer is, of course, the eternal preservation of the dead."[23]

Even the burial plots themselves are marketed based on the quality of experience—dare we say quality of life?—of the corpse. Mitford notes that in earlier periods the dead were buried on home plots in a rural setting, or in church yards or public cemeteries in urban settings. But by the twentieth century the for-profit cemetery had become the new normal. And with that for-profit status came a range of products with a range of prices. Her most extreme example is Forest Lawn in Los Angeles, where prices vary based on the quality of the view or the beauty of the gardens. She even found a premium tier with inspirational music piped in around the clock.[24]

Mitford's satire aims to expose the practices of funeral directors who prey on the grief, ignorance, and insurance-funded ready-cash of bereaved families who only want to do what's best for their loved ones. My interest is less in the corruption of funeral homes than in what her examples bring to light about the assumptions behind the marketing of these "artifacts."

In American culture, we put clothes on our dead as if they are alive. We place our dead in soft and sturdy coffins for comfort and protection as if they are alive. We manipulate their bodies and cover them in makeup and even set their faces with pleasant expressions so they look like they're alive. But the feet of the dead don't appreciate cushioned comfort. Their skin doesn't appreciate satin or lace. Their backs don't appreciate the warm reception of a foam mattress, and their eyes don't appreciate a beautiful view. "Thoughtfulness and consideration for the departed" is a

---

23. *Mitford, American Way of Death*, 37.
24. *Mitford, American Way of Death*, 85.

refusal to accept the departure. Underneath the appeal to comfort and preservation is a denial of the fundamental separation that has taken place. Behind the quest for a lifelike appearance is an attempt to deny the deathly reality.

Shameless: How We Talk about Death (or Don't)

One of Mitford's most ironic points is that among morticians mortality cannot be mentioned. *Death* is an unusable word. And any words that might suggest the ugly reality of death are carefully scrubbed out of the industry lingo. The corpse is not a "corpse." It's not even a "body." The corpse is Mr. Fill-in-the-Blank, or at the least, the Loved One. The death certificate isn't a death certificate—it's a "vital statistics form." The "funeral directors" (not morticians or undertakers) oversee the planning of "services" (not funerals) after which the "deceased" (not the dead) who have "expired" (not died) are "interred" (not buried) in "memorial parks" (not graveyards).[25]

The omission of death and its associations is not just another industry quirk in this quirky industry. It reflects what historian Philippe Aries calls a "brutal revolution": that death, "so omnipresent in the past that it was familiar, would be effaced, would disappear. It would become shameful and forbidden."[26] Aries describes how, in less than a century, a thousand years of precedent in how to think about, talk about, and experience death and dying has been swept away.

From the medieval period until the twentieth century death was a public phenomenon. The dying often knew when they were dying. There was no blind faith that medicine would make any difference, so medicine offered no excuse to avoid facing reality.

25. For these examples and more, see Mitford, *American Way of Death*, 51–53. Many of Mitford's examples come from a 1956 manual for funeral directors by Victor Landig: *Basic Principles of Funeral Service* (Houston: Scardino Print Co., 1956).

26. Philippe Aries, *Western Attitudes toward Death: From the Middle Ages to the Present*, trans. Patricia Ranum (Baltimore: Johns Hopkins University Press, 1974), 85.

Families, friends, and even children were familiar with death and didn't attempt to hide from it.

According to Aries, in the medieval West the deathbed scene was a public place. When folks on the street noticed a priest headed to offer last rites, they would fall in line behind him and process into the sickroom. As Aries puts it, "It was essential that parents, friends, and neighbors be present," including children.[27] Death was observed as a matter of course, and was no less public than birth or marriage.

Consider once again Christians living in colonial New England. There it was seen as virtuous to think and talk about death often. On their way to worship each Sunday they would have passed through a churchyard full of elaborate gravestones, put in place to remind them that they too would lie there in due time. Besides weekly sermons on Sundays, colonists would have heard occasional funeral sermons specifically aimed at death and how to prepare for it. They were regularly encouraged to meditate on death as a normal part of their devotional lives.

For example, Cotton Mather suggested turning the mundane details of life into triggers to think on death: "When we sit at our Tables, Let us think, I shall shortly be my self a morsel for the Worms. When we rest in our Lodgings, Let us think, A cold Grave will shortly be my Bed. And when we view the Chests, where we put our Treasures, Let us think, A little black Chest is that wherein I my self shortly may be Locked up."[28]

How do Mather's words land on you? Like nails on a chalkboard? Do they sound sick to you, perhaps even deranged? Before you lump in Mather's appeal with some sort of lunatic fringe, consider one more example. *The New England Primer* was a popular resource for educating children in eighteenth-century primary

---

27. Aries, *Western Attitudes toward Death*, 12.
28. Cited in Geddes, *Welcome Joy*, 65.

schools. One of its features helped students memorize the ABCs by matching each letter with a two-line rhyme and a picture inspired by the rhyme. So, for example, the *L* included a verse about the Lion and the Lamb. *Z* had a rhyme about Zacchaeus. So far so good. These rhymes sound much like our own—*A* is for alligator, *B* is for ball, *C* is for cat, and so on.

But among these general biblical characters was another common theme. The picture next to the letter *T* was a skeleton holding an hourglass in one hand and a reaper's scythe in the other. The verse: "Time cuts down all / Both great and small." The letter *X* reinforced the message, picturing an elaborately dressed figure on some sort of funerary pyre, with this rhyme: "Xerxes the great did die, / And so must you and I." The letter *Y* was still more jarring. The picture featured another skeleton, but this one was holding an arrow pointed down at the body of a small child. "Youth forward flips/Death soonest nips." They were teaching their children to read by reminding them they would die. As one historian put it, "The message to prepare to die came from so many sides that it was inescapable."[29]

By the mid-twentieth century these norms had shifted dramatically. And not just because most in the West now die in medical facilities rather than in their homes. The revolution is partly technological, but it's also much more. Death has not just become invisible, swept away into the alien world of hospitals, nursing homes, and assisted living facilities. Death has become unmentionable.

There are exceptions of course, but is it not true that if you admitted to thinking often of your own death you'd be labeled morbid? Or what if, over Thanksgiving dinner, you asked your father how he was feeling about his death in light of his stage 4

---

29. Charles Hambrick-Stowe, *The Practice of Piety: Puritan Devotional Disciplines in Seventeenth-Century New England* (Chapel Hill: University of North Carolina Press, 1982), 219. The *New England Primer* quotes are taken from Hambrick-Stowe's photo reproduction on 220–21.

cancer? Would it not seem at best impolite, at worst cruel? We don't often talk about death anymore. Why not?

Geoffrey Gorer, an English sociologist, was among the first to examine this roping off of death from polite conversation. In a groundbreaking essay called "The Pornography of Death," Gorer draws a telling analogy between the place of sex in the nineteenth century and the place of death in the twentieth century.[30] Even as the prominence of sex has broadened—in conversation, in mainstream television, in what kids are allowed to see and know—death has been shoved out of sight and out of mind.

In the 1870s, when death was everywhere, it would have been embarrassing to bring up sex at a dinner party. It would have been shameful to admit you think much about sex. It would have been irresponsible to talk to your kids about sex. But by the 1950s, when Gorer wrote, the taboo had shifted. Death had already become in the twentieth century what sex had been to the nineteenth century. In the nineteenth century adults told children that babies came when storks dropped them at the front door. Those same children stood bedside as their loved ones died. Now kids learn that grandpa's death means he's gone to a place where he can play golf or go fishing all day. Meanwhile, kids have 24/7 access to sexual content in their Instagram feeds.[31]

Perhaps at this point you're thinking, what taboo? If anything, our culture is obsessed with death, not avoiding the subject. In a sense you'd be right. Take for example how we entertain ourselves. Say some visitors from an alien world plopped down on an

30. Geoffrey Gorer, "The Pornography of Death," *Encounter*, October 1955, 49–52.

31. For these examples as an application of Gorer's point, I'm following the lead of Aries, *Western Attitudes toward Death*, 93. N. T. Wright, in *Surprised by Hope*, includes a more contemporary example from a children's book by Maria Shriver. Shriver describes the afterlife as a "beautiful place where you can sit on soft clouds and talk to other people who are there," and promises children that Grandma is "in a safe place, with the stars." Quoted in Wright, *Surprised by Hope: Rethinking Heaven, the Resurrection, and the Mission of the Church* (New York: HarperOne, 2008), 17.

average American sofa for a night of average American television. If they flipped on a local news broadcast in time for the lead story, chances are they'd hear of someone killed in a tragic traffic accident or perhaps a drive-by shooting or even a terrorist bombing. If they flipped over to drama, chances are they'd watch stories of people solving murders or people trying to save trauma patients or people trying to survive some sort of zombie apocalypse.

In the 2014–2015 season, seven of the top ten most-watched television programs in America were shows that centered on death. Take out comedy and football and the number is seven out of eight.[32] On Sunday nights, AMC's *The Walking Dead* continued its reign as the most-watched cable series in history, pulling nearly twenty million viewers and dominating the eighteen to forty-nine-year-old demographic. On weeknights, the most popular shows were crime dramas like *Criminal Minds* or *NCIS*. The cities vary a bit from show to show. Some protagonists are cops and others are military. But the core of each episode is pretty much the same: someone dies, and others have to figure out why. And this is just television. Browse any list of box office hits or best-selling video games and you'll find the same pattern.

With all this death on screen, can we really say that death has been pushed out of the public consciousness? Gorer would argue that it has, and this is the deeper insight of his essay. The fact that we're so drawn to death depicted the way it's normally depicted on screen actually proves the taboo status of death in our culture. It's evidence *for*—not *against*—our unspoken agreement to ignore the truth about death. Death may be common subject matter, but the message from our entertainment suggests death itself is anything but common.

---

32. Michael Schneider, "These Are the 50 Most-Watched TV Shows of the 2014–15 Season," TV Insider, June 3, 2015, http://www.tvinsider.com/article/1989/top-50-tv-shows-2014-2015-highest-rated-winners-and-losers/.

Think about it: the deaths shown in our most popular shows are violent deaths. They come to relatively young people who usually aren't expecting to die. Characters aren't dying of old age and natural decay. They're dying because a psychopath, a mafia hit man, or a zombie killed them. You don't watch these shows for insight into genuine human experience. You watch them to escape from genuine human experience. Shows like these, with deaths like these, are a guilty pleasure.

This insight is the backdrop for Gorer's essay title, "The Pornography of Death." When societies banish honest conversation about major aspects of human experience, the typical response is to compensate for ignorance of reality with self-indulgent fantasy. The depiction of death we consume in our popular culture is as far removed from natural death as pornography is from monogamous, married sexuality. In porn nothing about sex is real. The bodies aren't real, the settings aren't real, the physical exploits aren't real—it's all fantasy.

Pornographers aren't featuring couples faithfully married for ten or twenty years, working long hours at demanding jobs, so exhausted by their kids that they can barely function after nine p.m. In the same way, more often than not, where death shows up it belongs to a fantasy world. It's newsworthy. It's tragic. It's psychopathic or maybe apocalyptic. But one way or another, death is exotic. It's something that happens to someone else.[33]

Our experience of death on-screen, in other words, only reinforces our detachment from death in reality. All the while we move further and further from the death-awareness that came so naturally to Pascal. Think back to his image. He envisioned

---

33. Sigmund Freud noticed this tendency to emphasize the exotic: "We regularly stress the arbitrary nature of death, accident, illness, infection, old age, thus revealing our attempt to reduce death from an inevitability to chance," "Timely Reflections on War and Death," in *On Murder, Mourning and Melancholia*, trans. Shaun Whiteside (New York: Penguin, 2005), 184.

all of us living like condemned criminals awaiting execution. We stand at the end of the line as the sword falls on those in front of us one by one. Every death of every other person images our own, as our turn draws closer and closer. That's how he lived. When he saw death in general, it reminded him of his death in particular. But where death appears in our culture, its form is often perverse, distorted, impersonal, and detached from what is real. That's what happens when polite company banishes honest talk about hard truths.

Why Are We Avoiding the Truth about Death?

My goal in this book is the help us overcome our detachment from death so that we can enjoy a deeper attachment to Jesus. The chapters that follow aim to uncover the problem of death as a problem for every one of us in ways we experience but don't always recognize. But before re-engaging with death I want to conclude this chapter by answering an important background question: why has our culture been so intent upon and effective at removing death from our consciousness? Why, once medicine carved out space for us to avoid thinking about death, have we so thoroughly banished it from our minds? I see at least three factors.

Our Duty to Happiness

The first factor is that death doesn't sit well with our culture's obsession with happiness. We don't merely cling to our right to pursue happiness. We seem to believe that we have a right to the experience of happiness. This entitlement drives our surging consumer economy: if I'm not happy, I should buy something to make me happy. It drives our obsession with psychotherapy: if I'm not happy, I need a professional to figure out why and help me get there. But there is no consumeristic or therapeutic solution for the problem of death. There's no product you can buy that will bring back someone you love or add an extra year to your life. There's no therapeutic insight that could turn death into a good thing. The more you get to know yourself, even love yourself, the more deeply you grieve the end of yourself. We suppress death because it's an unanswerable challenge to our happiness.

Aries nailed this connection between suppression and happiness forty years ago. Aries describes happiness as a kind of moral duty. We act as if all of us have a "social obligation to contribute to the collective happiness by avoiding any cause for sadness or boredom, by appearing to be always happy, even if in the depths of despair." If happiness is a moral duty, grief is a moral failure. Aries continues: "By showing the least sign of sadness, one sins against happiness, threatens it, and society then risks losing its raison d'etre."[34]

Where happiness is a social obligation, grieving will always be antisocial behavior. At best, we'll view grief as a sickness that needs to be cured. At worst we'll view grief as offensive, maladjusted, and even shameful. Where happiness is a social obligation, "morbid" will always be a pejorative term. And those who speak freely of death and its effects will risk mockery, judgment, and alienation.

The Horrible Implications

A second factor brings us even deeper into the motives behind our avoidance of the truth about death. The reality is simply too horrible. Death cuts us off from everyone we love. It means the end to everything we enjoy about life. And it is a head-on assault against our dignity and significance as human individuals. Who can fully stand up under the weight of this knowledge? The irony is that in order to survive we must deny that we can't survive.

---

34. Aries, *Western Attitudes toward Death*, 93–94.

Early on in his Pulitzer Prize-winning *The Denial of Death*, psychologist Ernest Becker describes the knowledge of death as a uniquely human problem. Other animals don't have to worry about the implications of death. They fear it by instinct only, if at all. "They live and disappear with the same thoughtlessness: a few minutes of fear, a few seconds of anguish, and it is over. But to live a whole lifetime with the fate of death haunting one's dreams and even the most sun-filled days—that's something else." It's an impossible burden. Becker continues: "I believe that those who speculate that a full apprehension of man's condition would drive him insane are right, quite literally right."[35] For Becker, our denial of death is how we function normally. It's the only way to cope.

I believe there's a lot of truth to what Becker says. I don't buy the argument that familiarity with death makes death less threatening. That's how some have pushed back against our avoidance of the subject, as if, as medical historian Brandy Schillace argues, "once we meet death and keep it near, it ceases to threaten us, ceases to be alien."[36]

In many cases familiarity does take the sting out of something fearful. But with death I believe it's the other way around. I'm with novelist Julian Barnes, whose memoir details his lifelong fear of extinction with remarkable honesty.

Barnes admits he was at one time terribly afraid to fly because he didn't want to crash. Once, in his twenties, he was stuck overnight in the Athens airport waiting on a flight back to London. "To kill time," Barnes recalls, "I went up on to the viewing roof of the terminal building. From there, I watched plane after plane take off, plane after plane land. . . . I watched scores of planes not crash. And this visual, rather than statistical, demonstration of the safety of flying convinced me." Perhaps taking on a job with

---

35. Ernest Becker, *The Denial of Death* (New York: Free Press, 1973), 27.

36. Brandy Schillace, *Death's Summer Coat: What the History of Death and Dying Teaches Us about Life and Living* (New York: Pegasus, 2016), 11.

a mortuary or a hospice clinic would have a similar effect. The more you see of death the less troubling death becomes. That's essentially what Schillace and others suggest. But Barnes pinpoints the problem with this way of thinking. "The fallacy is this: at Athens airport, I was watching thousands and thousands of passengers *not* die. At an undertaker's or mortuary, I would be confirming my worst suspicion: that the death rate for the human race is not a jot lower than one hundred per cent."[37]

I believe Barnes is right. The truth about death is horrifying. The more you think about it, the more horrible it appears. To deny this is sentimentality. Avoiding the truth about death makes sense when there's nothing you can do to change it and no hope for deliverance.

That's also why Barnes's opening line makes sense: "I don't believe in God, but I miss him."[38] He understands what has been lost in the modern West where secularism holds such power. Admittedly his line isn't exactly a sincere one. He makes fun of himself for it as the book unfolds. But he's onto something. Death is an unshakeable cloud for those living in a closed universe, with no hope of a force from the outside breaking through to conquer for us what we can't conquer. With no hope of deliverance, death is too horrible to acknowledge.

The Christian Capitulation

This second factor, the intolerable implications of death, makes a third factor all the more tragic. The taboo our culture has imposed on all honest talk of death holds firm in part because we Christians have too often capitulated to the silence. Rather than emphasizing death as the backdrop for our gospel— a major reason for the goodness of Christianity and the hope it

---

37. Julian Barnes, *Nothing to Be Frightened Of* (New York: Vintage, 2008), 105–6.
38. Barnes, *Nothing to Be Frightened Of*, 3.

offers—we have all too often behaved as if death isn't inevitable or devastating.

We seek medical miracles no less aggressively than everyone else. In fact, a major 2009 study suggests we're even more likely than others to pursue every possible treatment, no matter how hopeless. In *The Art of Dying*, Rob Moll cites a study in the *Journal of the American Medical Association*, which found that "people of religious faith (95 percent of whom were Christians) were three times more likely to choose aggressive medical treatment at the end of their lives, even though they knew they were dying and that the treatments were unlikely to lengthen their lives."[39] Now of course there is nothing wrong with using the resources of modern medicine to extend life. Every second of life is a precious gift. So are these resources, by God's common grace. But the results of this study suggest we are at best no more realistic than the general public about the inevitability of death.

We pursue happiness on the same material terms as everyone else. And that makes death just as inconvenient a conversation topic. Consider, for example, the massive influence of the prosperity gospel. Where purveyors of the prosperity gospel are selling millions of books about your best life now, death will always be a taboo subject. The implications are not just sad; they're shameful.

In a *New York Times* op-ed, historian Kate Bowler describes why death is a particular kind of problem for the prosperity gospel. Bowler spent years studying leaders and individuals involved in the movement, then published her findings in one of the only academic books on the subject.[40] Barely two years after her book was published, Bowler was diagnosed with stage 4 cancer. In her

---

39. Rob Moll, *The Art of Dying: Living Fully into the Life to Come* (Downers Grove, IL: InterVarsity Press, 2010), 32.

40. Kate Bowler, *Blessed: A History of the American Prosperity Gospel* (New York: Oxford University Press, 2013).

op-ed, she offers powerful insight into why a Christianity defined by a quest for the blessings of life will have trouble thinking honestly about death.

According to Bowler, the power of the prosperity gospel rests in its simplicity as an explanation of why some do well in life and others don't. The good life follows from power of faith, the clarity of positive thinking, and the favor of God toward the obedient. It's cause and effect. It's all very straightforward and certain. But where does death fit into this view of life? What else if not failure of faith? Bowler gets the problem exactly: "The prosperity gospel holds to this illusion of control until the very end. If a believer gets sick and dies, shame compounds the grief. Those who are loved and lost are just that—those who have lost the test of faith." There is no graceful death in prosperity teaching. "There are only jarring disappointments after fevered attempts to deny its inevitability."[41]

Death, I've said, is a particular problem for prosperity gospel thinking, and the prosperity gospel for all its popularity is only one of many orientations within western Christianity. It would be overstating things to suggest that death has been banished from Christian conversations across the board. But still I wonder: when is the last time you heard a sermon preached about death, or heard the subject raised in a small group or a Sunday school class?

Finally, *I believe we often deny the pain of death like everyone else.* When faced with the death of others, we can talk as if every death is not a horrible, heartbreaking tragedy. I admit that at this point I'm drawing more from experience than hard numbers, but perhaps your experience matches mine. It seems to me our funerals can have our own version of the allergy to death Mitford described. We speak of our funerals as celebrations of life,

---

41. Kate Bowler, "Death, the Prosperity Gospel, and Me," *New York Times*, February 13, 2016.

not the chance to mourn the end of something beautiful or the hole left behind in a web of meaningful relationships. We remind each other that whatever is in the casket it isn't the one we loved. They're in a better place. Nothing to see here.

Of course there is some truth to these mantras. Heaven is central to our hope. And it's right that a Christian who has died in faith is in a better place. Paul tells us that to die is gain (Phil. 1:21), that to be absent from the body is to be present with the Lord (2 Cor. 5:8). All this is true and wonderful.

But think of Jesus's posture toward death (John 11:17–44). When he was confronted by the death of his friend Lazarus, he didn't tell Mary and Martha to remember that he's in a better place. He didn't come to Bethany for a funeral "celebration." Jesus wept. He was "deeply moved," even angry. He told them that he is the resurrection and the life, who came so those who believe in him would never die. And then he gave Lazarus's body new life.

Remember, too, that the same Paul who spoke of death as a kind of gain also called death the final enemy (1 Cor. 15:26). He said we're still waiting until that enemy should be made a footstool for Jesus's feet. For now the enemy still stands. Yes, death has already received a mortal blow. The death of death is as certain as the resurrection of Jesus. But death has not yet been swallowed up in victory.

When we Christians use Jesus as an excuse not to pay death much notice, we're guilty of what theologians call an over-realized eschatology. We're treating God's promises of a new world as if they've already come to pass—as if we're in present possession of all the gifts Christ came to purchase for us.

But this posture is no tribute to God's promises. Just the opposite in fact. When we act like death is no problem, we are not just being dishonest about the world as it is. We not only join our culture in denial and enable our collective self-deception. We also diminish what Jesus came to offer us and rob ourselves of the perspective from which his promises come alive.

What we experience now is a far cry from the tearless world we've been promised. Death is the separation of good things not meant to be sundered. It separates a person from family and friends. It separates the soul from its body and the body from the earth. Whatever joy may mark the current state of believers who have died, it is not what it will be, yet. Death is not ok. By avoiding the subject of death, we act like that's not true. And we shrink down the scale of Jesus's victory to fit the world we live in now.

The Bible's perspective on death is far more diverse and honest than merely a path to a better place. The chapters that follow explore the Bible's teaching on death and connect what it says to our experience. We have no reason to hide from the truth about death in all its ugliness. If death is not a problem, Jesus won't be much of a solution. The more deeply we feel death's sting, the more consciously we will feel the gospel's healing power. The more carefully we number our days, the more joyfully we'll hear that death's days are numbered too. And the more we allow ourselves to grieve the separations death brings to our lives, the more fully we will long for the world in which "he will wipe away every tear from their eyes, and death shall be no more, neither shall there be mourning, nor crying, nor pain anymore" (Rev. 21:4).

2

The Problem of Identity and the Promise of Union with Christ

Ivan Ilych thought he was too important to die. He was wrong, and so are we.

Ivan Ilych is the title character in one of Leo Tolstoy's most famous short stories, "The Death of Ivan Ilych," in which Tolstoy offers a powerful picture of how death exposes and demolishes our default self-centeredness.[1] When we first meet Ivan, his life is at its peak. He has a fine position at the Court of Justice. He's healthy, well-liked, wealthy, and successful. Mortality is far from his mind.

On one level, Ivan had learned the certainty of death in grammar school with a simple syllogism: Caius is a man. All men are

---

1. Leo Tolstoy, like so many other great fiction writers, was a man preoccupied by death throughout his life. He described his work as his attempt to compensate for his mortality, to create something meaningful that would overcome the power of his death. Death shows up in memorable ways throughout his work. For examples and a good introduction to the theme, see Mary Beard, "Facing Death with Tolstoy," *The New Yorker*, November 5, 2013, http://www.newyorker.com/books /page-turner/facing-death-with-tolstoy. For the following discussion I found the analysis of Victor Brombert very helpful: *Musings on Mortality: From Tolstoy to Primo Levi* (Chicago: University of Chicago Press, 2013), 13–24.

mortal. Therefore, Caius is mortal. He has no trouble acknowledging the reality of death-in-general. He just can't see death as part of his reality. To Ivan all of that was well and good for Caius, but that's Caius. That's not Ivan. Caius was some abstraction. Ivan's life was so concrete, so unique. "What did Caius know of the smell of that striped leather ball Vanya had been so fond of? Had Caius kissed his mother's hand like that, and did the silk of her dress rustle so for Caius?" Of course Caius had to die. But "for me, little Vanya, Ivan Ilych, with all my thoughts and emotions, it's altogether a different matter."[2]

Ivan can't imagine how a life like his, with such specific and unique and irreplaceable consciousness, could simply vanish. Then one day while Ivan is cleaning a window in his home, standing on a tall ladder, he slips and falls, suffering a mysterious injury that leads slowly but relentlessly toward his death. From this point most of the action takes place in his own head, as he comes to grips with what is happening to him. As his condition grows worse and worse, he realizes that practically no one cares about what is happening to him. He has become an inconvenience to family and friends. They have to break from their normal lives to visit him, and when they do, they talk about anything but what's happening to his body. Mostly he just lies there, alone and dying, listening to the sounds of his family—those to whom he thought he was too special to die—carrying on their lives without him.

As with the healthy Ivan Ilych, death feels to us like something that happens to other people. Our own death is unimaginable. It seems as if the world can't keep going without us. But the harsh reality of death tells another story. Death makes a statement about each of us: you are not too important to die. In this chapter, I want to help us feel the weight of death's challenge to

---

2. Leo Tolstoy, "The Death of Ivan Ilych," in *The Great Short Works of Leo Tolstoy*, trans. Louise and Aylmer Maude (New York: Harper and Row, 1967), 280.

who we are so that we can see the beauty and power of how God redefines us in Jesus. Otherwise, so long as death remains someone else's problem, Jesus will remain someone else's Savior.

Death Humbles Us: I Am Not Too Important to Die

It helps to recognize what death says about us if we think for a moment about what we say about ourselves, at least subconsciously. There's a narcissism in each of us that tells us the world can't go on without us.

Sigmund Freud argued that "in the unconscious each one of us is convinced of his immortality." If asked about it, of course we'd acknowledge we will die like everyone else. We would admit that the world will keep on spinning once we're gone. But imagine for a moment what your world would look like a week after you've died. What do you see? Perhaps your loved ones grieving, finding ways to cope without you? A fickle friend wishing he'd been nicer to you? Coworkers finally realizing they depended on you more than they ever knew? What you imagine isn't really the point. The point is that whatever you see, you're still the one seeing. When you try to imagine yourself as dead, you're still there, still surviving, as a spectator. So, Freud suggested, "Fundamentally no one believes in his own death."[3]

What Freud is getting at is that the world only exists for us as it is seen by us. It exists because we're here to see it and relate to it. Which is to say that, though we may not admit to it, at least subconsciously the world exists with us at its center. To shift the metaphor a bit, we're the sun around which everything else revolves.

In my world, though my mind concedes that Nashville has been around for more than two centuries, Nashville exists as my

---

3. Sigmund Freud, "Timely Reflections on War and Death," in *On Murder, Mourning and Melancholia*, trans. Shaun Whiteside (New York: Penguin, 2005), 183.

home. That's how I see it and relate to it. In a similar way, southwest Alabama exists as the place where I grew up. The Gulf Coast exists as a place I go with my family on vacation. And speaking of my family, Lindsey exists as my wife, Walter, Sam, and Benjamin exist as my children, and so on and so forth. You get the idea. We instinctively place ourselves at the center of things, and those things get their identity from how they relate to us. We can't imagine our death because we can't imagine anything without ourselves at the center.

Here's another way to put this idea: we all see ourselves as the lead character in the story of the world. In a book or a movie that tells the story of one central figure, other characters get their identity based on how they relate to the lead character. They fill their purpose as they weave into the story of the hero.

Take Robin Hood, for example. He's clearly the center of all the classic stories about him. Other characters set him up for the things he does. The king and the nobles are the ones from whom he steals money. The Sheriff of Nottingham is the villain, the one who tries to capture him and serves as the butt of his jokes. Little John, Friar Tuck, and the rest of the merry men are his friends, secondary characters who bring out his humor and help him when he's in trouble. Marion is the maiden who gives him someone to love and to rescue. All the characters get their roles from how they relate to Robin Hood.

Now, what we know about central characters is that they're too important to kill off. Other characters may come and go. Their deaths may even help to develop the story of the hero. They may give him reasons to grieve, or to feel regret, or to seek vengeance. But the hero can't die. If the hero dies, the story can't go on.

At least subconsciously, each one of us sees himself as the protagonist apart from which the story of the world can't go on. That's what Freud meant when he said we're all convinced of our own immortality. We see ourselves as indispensable. And this is the self-identification that death so ruthlessly exposes for foolishness. This is where death is so humbling. Death tells us we are not indispensable. We are not too important to die.

Not only will the world keep going without us—eventually we won't be remembered at all. The church I pastor meets just off the campus of a major university. Like similar colleges around the world, the campus is full of buildings named for indispensable people. A couple of years ago one of them was bulldozed to make room for a new facility bearing a new indispensable name. Here was a man influential enough to have a building named after him, a building that housed tens of thousands of students over the years, and yet I wonder, who remembers him now? I'm an alumnus and can't even remember the name on the building much less anything about who he was.

If that is true of a man who was important enough to have a building named after him, what about the rest of us? I think of the thousands upon thousands of native Americans who lived and died for century after century along the Harpeth River valley near my home. They left no written testimony. We know they existed because they left arrowheads, shards of pottery, scraps of bone. Their burial mounds dot the landscape near the river. We know they existed. But no one knows them as people. As fathers and mothers, sons and daughters, friends and lovers. As people. In a sense, it's like they never existed.

At some point, especially as you age, you must come to realize what Ivan Ilych did. Oblivion isn't just something that happened to someone else. It's happening to me, now. This awareness breaks into my consciousness every now and then with no discernible rhyme or reason. It hit me one day while driving with my oldest son that I didn't know my grandfather's father's name. My son asked me what it was, and I couldn't remember. That may not seem like a big deal at first blush, but consider the implications. My grandfather was a huge influence on my life. We named our oldest son after him. And my grandfather's father was surely a greater influence on his life than my grandfather had been in mine. But I couldn't remember his name. Now think forward a few steps. There's a good chance my son will have grandkids. Hopefully they will be precious to him, and he to them. But even if they are close to their grandfather (my son), they likely won't remember my name. It isn't only that they won't know what I was like, what I enjoyed, what others thought of me, what I accomplished, whom I loved—they won't even know my name. I won't be remembered by my own descendants in one hundred years.

Death Disorients Us: So How Important Am I?

The reality of death is profoundly humbling. It tells me that I'm not indispensable. It assures me I will be forgotten. And so death boots me from my self-appointed place at the center of the universe. But learning to recognize death's challenge to my subconscious narcissism also raises haunting questions about who I am. It isn't just that death is humbling. It can also be profoundly disorienting.

Most of us would probably agree that a reality check is a generally a good thing. No one likes a narcissist. Wouldn't it be better for all of us if none of us saw himself as more important than everyone else? If death puts us in our place, that's ultimately healthy, right?

Yes . . . *but*. Death's challenge actually pushes even deeper. Death's statement does more than put us in our place. It also raises questions about where our place actually is. Besides an organic mass that eats, sleeps, reproduces, and decomposes, who am I? What is the value of a life that doesn't even exist as someone's memory? So I'm not too important to die. Maybe I can accept that much. But if I'm dispensable, how important am I? Maybe I can see that the world doesn't revolve around me, but is it indifferent to me altogether?

Most of us assume that human lives matter. Every person has an identity shaped by unique experiences and interests and skills. We have relationships with people who love us and depend on us—people whose lives would be different without us. And because every person is unique, every person is irreplaceable and, therefore, precious. We typically just assume our importance as humans and spend our energy trying to distinguish ourselves from one another. We want to be exceptional, to rise above, to get ahead.

But death levels the winners and the losers, the rich and the poor, the popular and the outcasts—everyone. And if death is where we end up, we face a far greater question than whether we rise above our peers. The question isn't whether I distinguish myself from those I live around. The question is this: if my life turns to dust in the end, am I more significant than the stray dog picked apart by buzzards, the goldfish flushed down the toilet, or the cockroach crushed under foot?

Philosopher Luc Ferry describes how modern philosophers began to work out the problem of human significance after they had rejected the notion of a world created and ordered by any sort of deity. One central question drove this work: "What is the difference between men and animals?"[4] Without a creator to assign different values to different creatures, there has to be some other reason to believe that a human being has more worth than a possum or even a common housefly.

According to Ferry, Jean-Jacques Rousseau's answer was among the most influential. For Rousseau, the key difference between humans and animals is that humans have the ability

---

4. Luc Ferry, *A Brief History of Thought: A Philosophical Guide to Living* (New York: Harper, 2011), 103.

to rise above instinct. They can resist what comes naturally and make choices to be different than what they were.

A group of thinkers often called existentialists took Rousseau's ideas about human identity a few steps further. If what makes us human is our ability to rise above instinct, to make conscious and free choices about who we want to be, then human identity isn't something a human is born with. Rather, it's something we create for ourselves. You exist before you have an essence. There's a body before there's a you. You decide for yourself what makes your life significant.

Aspects of this philosophical case for human significance ring true. Surely this ability to rise above what comes naturally—to improve, to cultivate, to build culture—is a wonderful and unique characteristic of humanity. It is the ability behind laws protecting the weak from the strong. It's how neighboring countries avoid constant war. It enables great acts of altruism and beautiful works of art.

But if this ability to determine what and how to be is what makes humans different from animals, then death remains a devastating and arguably an unanswerable challenge. Ferry offers a helpful analogy of the problem. Let's say you have a magic wand that allows you by a simple wave to make the world so that everyone everywhere rises above instinct to respect one another, to put an end to violence and oppression, to build beautiful societies in which everyone is cared for, and to spend energy not in competition but in cultivation. "Suppose that, everywhere in the world, the rights of man were scrupulously observed, with everyone paying respect to the dignity of everyone else and the equal right of each individual to partake of those famous fundamental rights of freedom and happiness." That sounds good, right? What a wonderful place to live. Think of the effects: "There would be no wars or massacres, no genocide or crimes against humanity.

There would be an end to racism and xenophobia, to rape and theft, to domination and social exclusion, and the institutions of control or punishment—police, army, courts, prisons—would effectively disappear."[5] What a remarkable human achievement such a world would be. What a testimony to human ingenuity and willpower. "Yet," Ferry continues, "such a miracle would not prevent us from getting old, from looking on helplessly as wrinkles and grey hairs appear, from falling ill, from experiencing painful separations, from knowing that we are going to die and watching those we love die."[6]

We may claim that we matter because we decide who we are. We may insist that our will creates our identity, not nature, not instinct. Death makes a devastating counterclaim. Death says, in effect, go on and decide what to do with your life. Do something other than what an armadillo would do, or a carpenter bee, or a snail. Have fun with that. Just know that whatever you decide to be, whatever you decide to do, you cannot decide to be immortal. You still end up dead, just like the animals. In the end, no one resists nature. So, remind me, where do you get this idea that humans matter more than animals do?

Albert Camus, a French writer who lived 150 years after Rousseau, was among those who recognized that death shatters older notions of human significance. The "everyday man," Camus wrote in "The Myth of Sisyphus," lives his life "with aims, a concern for the future or for justification." This man "still thinks that something in his life can be directed. In truth, he acts as if he were free." But in light of death this freedom is no more than an illusion. The "freedom *to be* . . . ," Camus argued, ". . . does not exist. Death is there as the only reality."[7]

---

5. Ferry, *Brief History of Thought*, 134.

6. Ferry, *Brief History of Thought*, 135.

7. Albert Camus, "The Myth of Sisyphus," trans. Justin O'Brien, in *The Plague, the Fall, Exile and the Kingdom, and Selected Essays* (New York: Knopf, 2004), 538–39.

Camus is suggesting that death's effect on how we see ourselves in the world is far more than humbling. It should also be
profoundly disorienting. Awareness of death forces a tension
Camus called "the Absurd"—a clash between two realities that
seem undeniable. On one hand, we can't help living as if our lives
matter. We feel as if we as humans have a privileged place in the
world compared with other lives. We feel joined to the world, as if
its beautiful places and delicious foods and range of experiences
are meant for us to use and to enjoy. Dogs don't sit and gaze at the
colors of a sunset. Cats don't build high-rise condos with a view of
the coast and walkable beach access. Gerbils don't study physical
laws, master basic elements, and work with them to create technology, plan buildings, compose paintings. We live as if our relationship with the world as humans is special. The world feels like
a place where we are known, where our actions make a difference,
and where we are, if not indispensable, at least irreplaceable. It
may be nostalgia—that's how Camus refers to this orientation in
the world—but it's a strong and unshakeable nostalgia.

Then, in some moments, the consciousness of death breaks
in and disrupts this sense of order and familiarity. It forces
what Camus called "a confrontation between man and his own
obscurity."[8] When you recognize that you aren't central to the
world, that it will go on without you, that there's nothing unique
about where you end up, the world that had been small and hospitable, built around you and your expectations and desires,
now seems independent from you, inattentive and indifferent.
You may come to see yourself as a small speck in a vastness that
doesn't notice you. And with this consciousness comes, as Freud
put it, a feeling of estrangement from a world which once seemed
so beautiful and familiar.[9]

8. Camus, "The Myth of Sisyphus," 536.
9. Freud, "Reflections on War and Death," 183.

In other words, death-awareness can bring on a sense of alienation from the world. You see yourself detached from where you were once intimately united. This feeling of strangeness is highly subjective, of course. It varies from person to person, and it's difficult to put into words. Julian Barnes describes the startling effect of this awareness as similar to waking up to an alarm clock set by someone else: "At some ungodly hour you are suddenly pitched from sleep into darkness, panic, and a vicious awareness that this is a rented world."[10]

I find it easier to describe this feeling by analogy. For me, it feels something like what I imagine an astronaut feels floating in space. The movie *Gravity* has a horrifying scene where a person becomes detached from a space station and is floating alone and untethered in the vastness of space. The earth is often in frame but as a distant, small backdrop. Imagine yourself as that astronaut. From where you are, you can't make out your home country, much less your hometown. You can't see the streets of your neighborhood or the house that once draped over you like a warm blanket. You can't see the familiar and expected places that shrunk your world down to size and made it friendly and manageable. You see from here how small your world and its parameters have been. How small, therefore, you are.

Recognizing what death means for your identity can have this effect. It can make you feel unmoored, detached—as if you may as well be floating away, irrelevant and unnoticed. So far from being the world's center, you're not even at home there.

How Genesis Explains the Absurd

What does death have to do with our identity? Death humbles us, and death disorients us. Death tells us that we are not too important to die, that no one is indispensable. And with that

---

10. Julian Barnes, *Nothing to Be Frightened Of* (New York: Vintage, 2008), 24.

statement death confronts us with what Ernest Becker frames as our terrifying dilemma: "Man is literally split in two: he has an awareness of his own splendid uniqueness in that he sticks out of nature with a towering majesty, and yet he goes back into the ground a few feet in order blindly and dumbly to rot and disappear forever."[11]

There is a massive disconnect between what we feel about ourselves and what death implies about who we are. For Camus the disconnect is absurd. For Becker it's a dreadful dilemma. But for the Bible this disconnect goes right to the heart of death's origin and purpose. Death is not the natural end to a merely biological life. Death is an intrusion into the perfect world of the Creator designed by that same Creator to make a point. Death is a punishment for human pride. It exposes our foolish confidence in our freedom to be whoever we want to be.

Genesis explains the absurd by the twists and turns of a compelling story. Chapter 1 opens with a beautiful poem, almost a hymn to the Creator, describing God as the only reason that anything exists.[12] The world and everything in it exists because, in the beginning, when only God was, God created the heavens and the earth by his word (Gen. 1:1, 3). As the hymn unfolds, we follow him as he brings order and purpose from what was formless and void (1:2). He separates light from darkness and regulates both (1:4–5). He separates heaven from earth and then land from sea (1:6–10). Then he populates what he's ordered, filling up what was empty (1:11–25). He gives the sun, moon, and stars to distinguish darkness and light. He puts fish in the sea and birds in the air. He fills the land with plants and animals. Everything about

---

11. Ernest Becker, *The Denial of Death* (New York: Free Press, 1973), 26.

12. For the following discussion of Genesis 1–3, I depend on insights from Allen Ross, *Creation and Blessing: A Guide to the Study and Exposition of Genesis* (Grand Rapids, MI: Baker, 1998); Bruce Waltke, *Genesis: A Commentary* (Grand Rapids, MI: Zondervan, 2001); Gordon Wenham, *Genesis 1–15*, Word Biblical Commentary, vol. 1 (1987; Grand Rapids, MI: Zondervan, 2014).

this poem is meant to show God's creative power, his unrelenting purpose, and his absolute sovereignty. He speaks, and what he says happens, every time. Even the structure of the poem, and the symbolism of its words and numbers, points to the completeness of what God made. Everything was as he wanted it. Each stanza concludes with his benediction: he looked and saw that it was good (1:10, 12, 18, 21–25).

Genesis 1 celebrates God's absolute responsibility for everything that is, but this hymn also celebrates the unique dignity of humanity. The progression of the stanzas builds to the creation of man and woman, like the highest peak in a range of mountains. With the account of man and woman, the form of the passage shifts dramatically (1:26–31). Where preceding descriptions follow a tight formula, with rhythmic and repetitive language, with the man and woman the pattern is replaced by deliberation, fuller description, and even a kind of poem within the poem.

All creation testifies to God's beauty, creativity, and power. But humanity reflects him in an altogether unique way. Only the man and woman are created in his own image (Gen. 1:26). God looks with pleasure on every piece of his handiwork. At the end of each day, after every unique piece, he saw that it was good. But only over the man and the woman God pronounces his happiness: very good (1:31). And though the Scriptures tell us that every part of his world does his bidding, humanity alone receives God's commission to rule over and cultivate the creation on his behalf (1:26, 28).

Genesis 1 tells us that the dignity we feel is not an illusion. It isn't merely self-congratulation. According to the Bible, we were made to feel and to embrace the sanctity of human life. The fact that we're outraged by Auschwitz but hire cockroach exterminators isn't hypocrisy. It isn't boldfaced speciesism. It stems from the fact that human beings have a preciousness to their lives that cockroaches don't have. This is at the core of biblical anthropology, and it's the message of Genesis 1–2.

This perspective also explains why death is such an appalling, even unbelievable affront to what we know about ourselves. We sense the unique value of each human life. We're not merely interchangeable members of a set. Every person has memories, experiences, beliefs, affections, relationships, and all the rest that makes you *you*. In that sense every person *is* irreplaceable and sacred. How can that irreplaceable you simply be erased? It is a dreadful, mind-boggling, heartbreaking idea. And it feels dreadful to us, the Bible says, not because we're hardwired to overestimate our own value but because our instincts about human significance are mostly correct.

Mostly correct—an all-important qualifier. The Genesis account of our creation makes crystal clear another truth about human identity that is more difficult for us to accept. The dignity we feel is not an illusion. That much is true. But the dignity we possess—like the air we breathe—comes to us as a gift, undeserved, by the God who made us. It is always and only his image we bear. It is his Word alone that calls us very good. And it is his world we've been allowed to enjoy and charged to cultivate.

The death of every human is meaningful and tragic, theologian Helmut Thielicke says, because "it impinges upon an infinite and irreplaceable value. Something unique comes to an end." But according to Genesis, human lives "are unique and irreplaceable only under the Word." Our dignity is always and only what Thielicke calls an "alien dignity."[13] It covers us because God says so, but it's never fully ours. It belongs to God, and it's applied to us.

---

13. Helmut Thielicke, *Living with Death* (Grand Rapids, MI: Eerdmans, 1983), 152. For a fuller development of a similar argument, see Richard Lints's excellent and comprehensive account of the Bible's teaching on human identity in the image of God: *Identity and Idolatry:*

This is the point at which the story of humanity becomes a sad story—a story of distrust, of betrayal, and ultimately of death. Death enters the human story as an intrusion, something fundamentally unnatural. It isn't the conclusion of a life's cycle that has run its course. It is a punishment perfectly tailored to fit the crime of human sin.

So far I've argued that Genesis explains the dignity we feel—one-half of our absurd dilemma. But ours is a created dignity. It's a derived, gifted dignity. It is the dignity of the moon catching the light of the sun. And it has never been enough for us. Perhaps you've heard of Aesop's fable of the dog who catches his reflection on the surface of the water. He already has a nice bone, but as soon as he sees what looks like another bone, in the mouth of the dog in the water, what he has already isn't enough anymore. He grabs for the mirage only to lose his grip on the bone he had. It's a helpful image for the way the Bible describes the origin of death. Every human who has ever lived would rather be the sun than reflect its light. We would rather be God than rest content in his image. All of us would rather play the lead role in the history of the world. But to assert our own identity rather than receive it from God is to lose ourselves altogether in death.[14]

This story plays out in Genesis 3. In Genesis 2 God has given his image bearers instructions for their unique role in the world. He has also warned them to remember their place—to trust his provision and to honor his commands. "You may surely eat of every tree of the garden, but of the tree of the knowledge of good and evil you shall not eat, for in the day that you eat of it you shall surely die" (Gen. 2:16–17). God is warning them: Disobey my

---

The Image of God and Its Inversion (Downers Grove, IL: InterVarsity Press, 2015). Lints argues, "Human identity is rooted in what it reflects" (30).

14. Richard Lints's framing is helpful: "The irony of identity is that by looking away from ourselves we are more likely to discover our identity." We are "created as people who find their identity in their capacity to reflect the Creator and the created order" (*Identity and Idolatry*, 11).

words, and you will die. Try to define your life for yourself, and you'll lose your life.

Genesis 3 opens on an ominous note. The first verse introduces a new character in the story, a serpent more crafty and devious than any other creature. He is the first to challenge the authority of God's Word. To this point God's Word has been irresistible. He speaks, and worlds come to be. Nothing and no one hesitates to do exactly what his Word decrees. But the serpent casts shadows on that same authoritative word. "Did God *actually* say . . ." (Gen. 3:1)? He sounds like a child trying to wiggle out from under the command of a parent, pushing boundaries, shifting interpretations.[15]

In the end the serpent explicitly reverses what God precisely warned. "You will not surely die" (Gen. 3:4). Do not miss the subtext in this seductive assurance. You will not surely die. You can't die. You're too important to die. The show can't go on without its lead. Who would keep watching, and why would they watch? Don't worry about death. Just focus on the next step. Don't you want to be like God?

The story of the fall is the story of Adam and Eve trading an identity given them by God for an alternative of their own design. The awful results follow immediately. The first sign of death is their insecurity. They feel guilty, ashamed, and fearful (Gen. 3:7). They are disoriented in a world that had been home to them, peaceful and familiar. They know themselves to be separated now, from the one who was their only source of life, dignity, and purpose (3:8–10). Death's shadow has already fallen over their lives. The death of their bodies would only complete the dissolu-

---

15. In fact, God did not say what the serpent quotes. He didn't prohibit eating from any tree; he named one specific tree off limits (Gen. 2:17). But the seed of doubt is there now, for Eve, and she builds on it. Her response to the serpent even shifts the nature of God's command. She adds to it: don't touch. And she takes away from it: "you will surely die" becomes "lest you die" (Gen. 3:3). See Ross, *Creation and Blessing*, 134–35.

tion of their identities that has already begun. They don't know who they are or where they stand.

Death is a punishment perfectly fitted to the offense. It tells us we are not the center of the universe. We are not indispensable. The world will go on without us. We are not too important to die. Death makes a statement about who we are, and the Bible tells us that's its whole purpose. The dignity we feel and the indignity of death aren't in absurd contradiction. The tension comes not from some mistake in an evolutionary code. The dignity we feel is real. But death shows it doesn't belong to us.

How the Gospel Resolves the Absurd

The Bible explains what Camus found to be absurd—the contradiction between the dignity we feel and the obscurity we face in death. Thanks be to God, the Bible also offers a better way forward.

How do you face up to a life that's defined by death? Camus suggested two main options. One was suicide. He suggested that the fundamental question of all philosophy is whether or not suicide is necessary. Should I go on toward death, drawing out the inevitable, or put an end to my life now? I can't choose whether my life will have any meaning. It won't. But at least I'm free to choose when my life ends. That's one option.

Camus preferred a second option, though. Something he called revolt.[16] Live *as if* you matter. Live in denial of death. Pretend that your life and the lives of those you love have value that death won't erase. As an act of protest against death, live your life with dignity and purpose.

This sort of denial is probably the most common way to cope with death's implications. But it's dishonest. It means living a lie. And even worse than the dishonesty, this denial leaves our

---

16. Camus, "The Myth of Sisyphus," 536–37.

self-centeredness unchecked. It carves out space for me to keep on living as if I'm the center of the universe and everyone else is merely plugging into my story.

The gospel offers a liberating, life-giving alternative to denial and despair. There is no need for denial: death's implications for who we are provide the crucial backdrop for the work of Christ. And there is no need for despair: union with Christ radically transforms who we are.

We must hear and accept the statement death makes about who we are before we can fully rejoice in the message of the gospel. Death says you are less important than you've ever allowed yourself to believe. The gospel says you are far more loved than you've ever imagined. You are not too important to die. But you are important enough that God gave his only begotten Son, so that if you believe in him you will not perish but have eternal life (John 3:16).[17] You will not be defined by death.

We must tread carefully if we are to see the gospel in all its beauty. An awareness of death that won't shrink back from the truth can help us to check our inner narcissism and rest in the promises of God. The gospel, seen in the light of what death means for us, tells us we are important because we are loved, not loved because we're important. God's love initiates, marks us off, redefines who we are.

So long as we see ourselves as the central character in the story of the world, the core concepts of the gospel will seem abstract, unnecessary, maybe even off-putting. Before I face up to the truth about death and the truth about myself, my inner narcissism goes unchecked. I continue to see myself as the center of the universe. I identify everyone else, including God, in light of

---

17. I'm adapting a helpful gospel summary by Tim Keller: "The Christian gospel is that I am so flawed that Jesus had to die for me, yet I am so loved and valued that Jesus was glad to die for me. This leads to deep humility and deep confidence at the same time" (*The Reason for God* [New York: Dutton, 2008], 181).

how they fit with my story. God is not the center of all things, the one from whom and through whom and to whom all things exist. God is a secondary character defined by how he comes into my story. So, if I need saving, of course God will save me. Who is God? God is the one who loves and protects me. That's his role to play. That's how he fits into this story that centers on me.

When we make God into a bit character who props up our lead—when we flatten out his character to fit the constraints of our story—much of the gospel's message will remain difficult to understand, much less love. The fact that God would love us makes sense. But why does the Bible speak so often of sacrifice and sin and grace and mercy? Why is there so much blood involved? What makes atonement necessary? Those concepts can devolve to mere words we recite without understanding, much less affection. They make God seem distant, foreign even—certainly not approachable, not immanent, not loving.

But when I hear what death says about me, I begin to see that I'm not the center of the universe after all. I'm a usurper who deserves to be put in his place. I begin to see that God is the only lead in this story, that I'm a character in a story that's about him. Only when I see his glory, and recognize that I am utterly dispensable, am I prepared to be amazed by the message of the gospel. Only then can I see and taste why it's wonderfully *good* news.

Gospel Identity: The Promise of Union with Christ

To be a Christian is to be "in Christ." This union with Jesus is at the core of the gospel, a catchall for the benefits of salvation. It's a theme Paul returns to again and again throughout his letters.[18] And to be one with Christ is to take on an altogether different identity, to become a new creation. Here's how Paul puts it in

---

18. Marcus Johnson identifies approximately 164 references to union with Christ in Paul's letters alone, not to mention many similar phrases in the writings of John. See *One with Christ: An Evangelical Theology of Salvation* (Wheaton, IL: Crossway, 2013), 19.

2 Corinthians 5:17: "Therefore, if anyone is in Christ, he is a new creation. The old has passed away; behold, the new has come." In his letter to the Colossians, he reminds us that we have "put off the old self" and have "put on the new self": "Here there is not Greek and Jew, circumcised and uncircumcised, barbarian, Scythian, slave, free; but Christ is all, and in all" (Col. 3:9–11). To be in Jesus and to have Jesus in you means that what once defined you has been replaced. You are a new creation. And your identity is now defined by Jesus. What is true of him is true of you.

When Paul wrote of this identity transformation, he wrote from experience. In Philippians 3 he describes his own former identity. He lists the things about himself that he used to value, the things about his birth and his character and his accomplishments that once gave him "confidence in the flesh" (Phil. 3:4). But now all these things, everything that once defined him, Paul counts "as rubbish, in order that I may gain Christ and be found in him, not having a righteousness of my own that comes from the law, but that which comes through faith in Christ, the righteousness from God that depends on faith—that I may know him and the power of his resurrection, and may share his sufferings, becoming like him in his death, that by any means possible I may attain the resurrection from the dead" (3:8–11).

What does it mean to "gain Christ"? Who are you when you're "found in him"? We could spend our whole lives meditating on the benefits of union with Christ and not reach the end of its life-giving relevance. But two aspects of this union directly confront death's challenge to who we are.

I want to focus on justification and adoption.[19] Both concepts relate to identity, to who you are as God defines you. When we

---

19. For justification and adoption as central to union with Christ, see Michael Horton, *The Christian Faith: A Systematic Theology for Pilgrims on the Way* (Grand Rapids, MI: Zondervan, 2011), 620–47. See also Johnson, *One with Christ*, chaps. 3 and 5.

view these concepts through full awareness of what death says about us, what may have once seemed sterile and colorless appears vibrant and beautiful. Because of our sin, death defines us as guilty, dispensable, and alienated in the world. Because of Christ, through justification, God defines us as innocent, worthy, even pleasing to him. And through adoption, the children of dust become children of God.

Justification: When You Are One with Christ, You Are Righteous

In Philippians 3 "righteousness" is Paul's first example of what you gain when you're found in Christ (v. 9). It isn't a word we use often in normal conversation, but for Paul it was crucial. It appears again and again throughout his letters. But in Romans he offers perhaps his most complete description of this righteousness and what it means to be justified through faith in Christ.

The first five chapters of Romans make up one long argument about justification. At root, it's an argument about human identity: who are we, really? In chapters 1–3 Paul points to the created world, to the human conscience, and to the law of God to make one devastating point: "None is righteous, no, not one" (Rom. 3:10). No one is who he should be before God.

Paul knows the human heart. We are relentless self-justifiers. We are always explaining ourselves—why we think the way we think, why we do the things we do, why we want the things we want. And usually we explain ourselves in order to distinguish ourselves. We want to be a cut above. We want visible evidence that we are the superior specimens we believe ourselves to be.

But Paul punctures our pretensions and levels our self-made hierarchies with one simple summary: "All have sinned and fall short of the glory of God" (Rom. 3:23). His words echo with the message we've heard in Genesis. Rather than embracing our dignity in God's image, we exchange his glory for a cheap copy of our own design. Who am I? Paul tells me: I am a sinner. I am guilty.

Then, against this bleak backdrop, Paul unveils his beautiful and unexpected portrait of the gospel, what Leon Morris calls "possibly the most important single paragraph ever written":[20]

> For all have sinned and fall short of the glory of God, and are justified by his grace as a gift, through the redemption that is in Christ Jesus, whom God put forward as a propitiation by his blood, to be received by faith. This was to show God's righteousness, because in his divine forbearance he had passed over former sins. It was to show his righteousness at the present time, so that he might be just and the justifier of the one who has faith in Jesus. (Rom. 3:23–26)

When Paul says that sinners are "justified," he uses an image from a court of law. To be justified is to be declared innocent. Justification is a sentence, pronounced over the one who is accused, that defines who he is: not guilty.

But it is far more than a statement of what a person hasn't done. In Christ we aren't only declared innocent. We are also declared righteous. We are approved. We are affirmed. A justified person is what he should be: worthy, because he's pleasing to God. To be justified is to be, in C. S. Lewis's phrase, "a real ingredient in the divine happiness."[21] The life of the justified person is a life of immense value because it is a life that brings God glory.

That means justification is far more than a cold legal formula. Justification is God's radical endorsement of every person who is in Christ. It is his affirmation of the person's significance—the

---

20. Leon Morris, *The Epistle to the Romans* (Grand Rapids, MI: Eerdmans, 1988), 173.

21. C. S. Lewis, "The Weight of Glory," in *The Weight of Glory* (1949; New York: Harper, 2001), 39.

significance we were made to crave. The life of the justified person is necessary and indispensable not because it's central to the universe, but because it's beloved by the God *who is* at the center of the universe.

Now think of justification as God's answer to death's statement about our lives. Death humbles us, but justification exalts us. On our own, no matter what we make of ourselves, death always writes the epitaph: dispensable. But when your life is hidden with Christ? When your name is graven not on a headstone that will crumble or even a building that will be replaced, but on his hands? Then God the justifier looks on you and says: worthy. Not an inch short of my glory. Facing death with honesty, you have to ask, what is the value of my life if it ends like this? Joined with Christ, the righteous one, God looks on you and answers: pleasing to me, and therefore precious.

Death has no answer for God's justifying word, no claim on a life that is worthy. "There is therefore now no condemnation for those who are in Christ Jesus. For the law of the Spirit of life has set you free in Christ Jesus from the law of sin and death" (Rom. 8:1–2). In Christ—and only because of Christ—you are not who you were. You are no longer dispensable. And God will not let death hold the last word against the righteous: "If the Spirit of him who raised Jesus from the dead dwells in you, he who raised Christ Jesus from the dead will also give life to your mortal bodies through his Spirit who dwells in you" (8:11).

Adoption: When You Are One with Christ, You Are a Child of God

Through the beginning of Romans 8 Paul unfolds the beauty and benefits of justification, with death as his backdrop for the promise of life in Christ. In chapter 5 he contrasts identity in Adam, who brought death to all, with identity in Christ, who spreads life to all. In chapter 6 Paul draws from the imagery of baptism to argue that "if we have been united with him in a death like his, we shall certainly be united with him in a resurrection like his" (Rom. 6:5). And everything builds to his summary celebration in 8:1: "There is therefore now no condemnation for those who are in Christ Jesus."

Then, midway through Romans 8, Paul's focus shifts to another benefit of God's salvation in Christ, and with that benefit a new image for the believer's union with Jesus. Paul introduces the promise of adoption. Joined to Jesus we are sons and daughters of God. Like justification, it's an image that directly confronts death's challenge to who we are. Through justification, God exalts those whom death had brought low. He gives dignity and purpose to those whose lives were otherwise dispensable. Through adoption, God gives security and belonging to those whom death had disoriented. Just as death's statement about our identity, when we learn to read it, creates an existential crisis, so God's statement over us in Christ creates over time an existential peace, wholeness, and security.

Immediately after showing that death has no claim on those who are in Christ, Paul celebrates the new status in God's family for all who believe. The same Spirit who binds us to Christ's righteousness also makes us children of God. The new legal reality comes with a new experience of life in the world: "For you did not receive the spirit of slavery to fall back into fear, but you have received the Spirit of adoption as sons, by whom we cry, 'Abba!' 'Father!'" (Rom. 8:15).

Through death we may as well be nameless. We're essentially waiting to be forgotten in time. But in Christ we are known, eternally, by the Father with the same intimacy and affection he has for his Son (see Eph. 1:3–5). We wait, still, but not to be forgotten. We wait as "fellow heirs with Christ" for the time when our inheritance will be revealed. Paul says all creation waits with us, groaning as if in childbirth, longing for the day when we will be free from decay and our bodies will be redeemed (Rom. 8:17, 19–23).

Paul is describing a world that is not yet what it should be. Decay is still our reality. The inheritance has not yet been given. But he argues that those who are in Christ experience this world of decay with the hope of children who belong to a powerful Father. Yes, they hope for what they do not see. But they wait for it with patience. Because in Christ they do not experience decay and death alone. They cry "Father!" with the knowledge that he "who did not spare his own Son but gave him up for us all" will now "with him" give them everything they need (Rom. 8:32).

Now reflect on Paul's assurance in light of the disorienting effect of death we discussed earlier. Recall the image from *Gravity*: a solitary person floating in space, unmoored, while the world below spins on, silent and indifferent. When we recognize that life is fragile and fleeting, the world that once seemed like home appears strange to us, unfamiliar and even hostile. We feel small and unprotected. Facing up to death, it makes sense to wonder: Where do I belong?

Paul's celebration of adoption in Christ might as well be framed as an answer to this question. Death disorients us, alienating us from each other, from the world, and even from our own bodies. Our adoption reorients us. It assures me that the Creator and Ruler over this and every other world has the specific and vigilant concern for me of a loving Father for a precious son. He is not indifferent. He knows me with intimate, discriminating knowledge. He invites me to cry to him at will—Abba! And he promises I am not unmoored, drifting, rootless, and alone but rather wrapped up, embraced, and engulfed by his powerful, protecting love. What can separate us from the love of God in Christ (Rom. 8:35, 39)? Nothing.

Granted, there is no promise that we will always experience the world as a hospitable and friendly place, always bending to our expectations and desires. The world remains for now in bondage to decay, groaning for deliverance. So much of what happens to us is obviously out of our control. And it can seem like we are at the mercy of forces absolutely indifferent to us. Paul assumes our experience will include nakedness and trial and violence and distress and danger (Rom. 8:35). We don't get reoriented to the world by embracing any naive assumptions of its innocence or goodness.

We are reoriented instead by the love of our Father. To be in Christ is to be a child of the one who rules over all and makes all things work together for the good of those who love him (Rom. 8:28).

Recently our family made a brief visit to London. We had only a few days to cram in as many neighborhoods and parks and museums and toy stores and restaurants as we could manage. We forced our way through immense crowds on sidewalks and subways and buses. The city wasn't familiar to me. It might as well have been another planet to my two small boys. On their own they were completely lost. They were a couple of tiny faces in a crowd of millions with no one paying them much attention. They were subject to a host of dangers they couldn't even imagine. But they were joyful, free, and excited because they were oriented to me. My presence, my hands holding theirs, shrunk the world down to size for them. Our relationship grounded them. They could rest in my knowledge and power and protection. They knew their place and even felt at home through relationship with me.

Reoriented through relationship. That is the gospel's answer to death's disorienting challenge. Whatever difficulties our experience of the world may include, however unfamiliar, cold, even hostile it may seem at times, we know our place. We are children of God. In Christ, we belong with him. "For," Paul concludes,

"I am sure that neither death nor life, nor angels nor rulers, nor things present nor things to come, nor powers, nor height nor depth, nor anything else in all creation, will be able to separate us from the love of God in Christ Jesus our Lord" (Rom. 8:38–39).

What do we gain when we are found in Christ? We gain exactly what death shows us we need. We gain a Father. We gain a belonging as secure and immovable as the powers of heaven. We gain the promise of an inheritance waiting to be revealed. Death has no lasting claim on the children of God.

Death-Awareness and Joy in the Gospel

In this chapter I've tried to show that we must face up to what death says about us if we want to rest in what God says about us in Jesus. In other words, the path to the gospel identity of Romans 8 must run through the honest desperation of Romans 7. I appreciate how Walter Wangerin makes this connection in *Mourning into Dancing:* "'Wretched man that I am!' cries Paul, and so must we. We must more than admit it by the mouth; we must suffer in fact our essential impotence, in order next to cry: 'Who will deliver me from this body of death?'"[22]

Who will deliver me? There it is. That's the right question. That's the only question left when we confront death's challenge with honesty. When we experience death's dark shadow, we are prepared to see the light that comes next. "All else has failed in death," Wangerin writes. "Everything of self was proven useless through grief. One name alone endures. It is now not merely a doctrine; it is experience; it is with genuine joy that I shout out loud: 'Thanks be to God through Jesus Christ our Lord! For the law of the Spirit of life in Christ Jesus has set me free from the law of sin and death!'"[23]

---

22. Walter Wangerin, *Mourning into Dancing* (Grand Rapids, MI: Zondervan, 1992), 122.
23. Wangerin, *Mourning into Dancing*, 122.

We must allow death-awareness to break down life-on-our-terms before we will ever connect with the promise of new life in Christ. We must watch wide-eyed as death strips away our illusions—our self-love, self-importance, and self-justification. Death means the end of our old selves. Only by embracing this reality are we prepared to put on the new self—an identity not of our design or accomplishment but of God's free gift and based on Jesus's accomplishment. But that is a wonderful and blessed exchange. "What am I now if not a god?" Wangerin asks, given the grief and sober self-awareness death imposes. "Oh, dear Jesus—I am a child. Helpless, needy, weak, returning to thee, and by thee to the kingdom of heaven! I am the prodigal, come to myself and coming home again."[24]

---

24. Wangerin, *Mourning into Dancing*, 147.

3

The Problem of Futility and the Promise of Purpose

About fifteen years ago social commentator Gregg Easterbrook wrote an insightful book called *The Progress Paradox: How Life Gets Better while People Feel Worse*.[1] Focusing on America, he shows that in many significant ways quality of life has improved dramatically over the last half-century. And this has been true for the majority of people, not just the uber-wealthy. He points to homeownership, the average size of living quarters, even the comfort of those living quarters. At the time Easterbrook wrote, roughly 95 percent of people enjoyed central heat, compared with just 15 percent two generations earlier. He points to increased access to health care and to the ability of health-care providers to fight disease and ease discomfort. He points to improved work conditions, an overall decrease in work hours, and a corresponding rise in leisure

---

1. Gregg Easterbrook, *The Progress Paradox: How Life Gets Better while People Feel Worse* (New York: Random House, 2003). I found my way to this book through Philip Ryken, *Ecclesiastes: Why Everything Matters* (Wheaton, IL: Crossway, 2010).

opportunities. He also notes the disposable income many are able to spend on leisure activities: in 2001, Americans spent roughly $25 billion on recreational watercraft.[2]

Most Americans enjoy a quality of life that would have been unimaginable for even the wealthiest Americans two hundred years ago. But after all this time, even with all this progress, happiness hasn't risen in tandem. In fact, Easterbrook shows that clinical depression "has been rising in eerie synchronization with rising prosperity," roughly ten times the diagnosed cases of fifty years ago.[3]

Why is it that no matter how much we have, no matter how good we have it, we struggle to feel satisfied? Why do we so often feel let down? What would it take for us to be fulfilled?

In this chapter I'll be referring to this experience of dissatisfaction, disappointment, or unhappiness as the problem of futility. And I will trace this problem to its common but unnoticed source. William James described death as the "great specter" underneath everything, the "worm at the core" of everything we look to for happiness.[4] If we want to cope with futility, we must understand where James is coming from. We must learn to see the power of death behind our frustration with life. This chapter is about what death does to the things we look to for meaning and purpose—the things we hope to enjoy, to accomplish, to acquire. We must come to recognize that, left to ourselves, everything is

---

2. For these examples and many more, see Easterbrook, *Progress Paradox*, 3–50.

3. Easterbrook, *Progress Paradox*, xvi.

4. William James, *The Varieties of Religious Experience: A Study in Human Nature*, The Modern Library (1902; New York: Random House, n.d.), 136–38. James introduces an extended quote from Ecclesiastes with this insight: "Make the human being's sensitiveness a little greater, carry him a little farther over the misery-threshold, and the good quality of the successful moments themselves when they occur is spoiled and vitiated. All natural goods perish. Riches take wings; fame is a breath; love is a cheat; youth and health and pleasure vanish. Can things whose end is always dust and disappointment be the real goods which our souls require? Back of everything is the great spectre of universal death, the all-encompassing blackness" (136). For a full exploration of James's insight by a team of psychologists, see Sheldon Solomon, Jeff Greenberg, and Tom Pyszczynski, *The Worm at the Core: On the Role of Death in Life* (New York: Random House, 2015).

meaningless because everyone dies. Only then are we prepared to see how everything is meaningful because Jesus is alive.

Recognizing Futility in Life

> I the Preacher have been king over Israel in Jerusalem. And I applied my heart to seek and to search out by wisdom all that is done under heaven. It is an unhappy business that God has given to the children of man to be busy with. I have seen everything that is done under the sun, and behold, all is vanity and a striving after wind. (Eccles. 1:12–14)

Unless you've read Ecclesiastes before, you may be surprised to learn the Bible speaks like this. These words are the opening summary of a book that is relentlessly dark in its view of life, sometimes shocking in its despair, and seemingly nihilistic in places. It's a meditation on vanity or meaninglessness that would fit just as well among French existentialists as it did in its Hebrew setting.[5]

One reason its message seems timeless is that Ecclesiastes belongs to a genre known as wisdom literature. Wisdom in the Bible isn't about intelligence. You can't get wise by memorizing lots of facts. Wisdom is more like a skill you acquire through observation and practice. It's an instinct for living well in the world as it is. And wisdom never pretends things are better than they are. It never shrinks back from acknowledging the harsh realities of life.

Ecclesiastes fits within this wisdom literature as a powerful warning: even if you manage your life well, even if you take all the right opportunities and reach all of your goals, what you

---

5. *Hebel*, the Hebrew word often translated "vanity" or "meaningless," literally refers to a breath of air or a vapor. Metaphorically, it refers to transience, emptiness, what is lacking in substance. It's a way of describing futility. The word occurs more than thirty times throughout the book's twelve chapters, something of a motto for the Preacher's perspective. See Derek Kidner, *The Wisdom of Proverbs, Job and Ecclesiastes: An Introduction to Wisdom Literature* (Downers Grove, IL: InterVarsity Press, 1985), 90.

end up with will never be enough. When you're young, it's easy to assume you're not happy because you haven't yet arrived. But the older you get, the more often you arrive and feel let down, the more you realize that what you thought you wanted isn't really what you want. The Preacher of Ecclesiastes knows this from experience. He was a man who had everything and found it still wasn't enough. And you may be surprised how his experience, like the beam of a high-powered spotlight, illuminates your own. You'll soon see why this book has been called "the most contemporary book in the Bible."[6]

Work

The opening chapters of Ecclesiastes read like the journal of a scientist tracking his experiments. The Preacher is testing the good things of life, looking for anything that matters—anything more lasting and fruitful than a striving after wind.

His first subject is work. It makes sense that he would begin here. Our work consumes a tremendous amount of our time, our energy, and our mental space. In one way or another, our work is the object of some of our greatest hopes for our lives. But, the Preacher asks, "What does a man gain by all the toil at which he toils under the sun?" (Eccles. 1:3). By the time he repeats the question in 2:22, he has made a detailed case for the futility of everything we do under the sun. His answer is not pleasant. But it is a powerful assessment of what drives us, and frustrates us, in our work. The opening question leads straight into a poem on creation:

> The sun rises, and the sun goes down,
>> and hastens to the place where it rises.
> The wind blows to the south
>> and goes around to the north;

---

6. See Sidney Greidanus, quoting Leland Ryken, in *Preaching Christ from Ecclesiastes* (Grand Rapids, MI: Eerdmans, 2010), 2.

around and around goes the wind,
  and on its circuits the wind returns.
All streams run to the sea,
  but the sea is not full;
to the place where streams flow,
  there they flow again. (Eccles. 1:5–7)

Psalm 19 views the rising and the setting of the sun as everyday evidence for God's sustaining power and loving care for what he has made. Job 38 sees the limits of the oceans as a result of God's authority to hem them in by his Word. The Preacher draws a different conclusion: "All things are full of weariness; a man cannot utter it" (Eccles. 1:8). The same features of the world that inspire praise in one case cause weariness here. Why?

Remember, his examples from nature come in answer to a question about the value of work. He uses the repetitiveness in creation to symbolize the futility of our work. He's complaining about monotony. Everything just keeps going, day after day, while our lives come and go.

The Preacher is highlighting one of the common motives for our work: a sense of accomplishment. The satisfaction of a job well done. The joy of tracing one's progress from beginning to end, like watching a yard mowed row after row until it's finished. There is a powerful sense of relief that comes when a project is completed, or when the last box on the list is checked off. But there is another side to work that you must admit, whether you work as a professional or as a student or as a mother of young children: your work is never, ever done. Every day brings new responsibilities. There will always be more papers to write, more reports to file, more clothes to wash or floors to mop or meals to prepare for and clean up after. One project always leads to another. So what is gained, really?

The repetitiveness of nature points to one more problem with work that's at least as disappointing for us. We work to make a mark, to do something valuable, something noticeable, something that makes a difference. But more often than not things stay the same. Ultimately nothing changes. No one notices. And no one will remember.

> What has been is what will be,
>> and what has been done is what will be done,
>> and there is nothing new under the sun.
> Is there a thing of which it is said,
>> "See, this is new"?
> It has been already
>> in the ages before us.
> There is no remembrance of former things,
>> nor will there be any remembrance
> of later things yet to be
>> among those who come after. (Eccles. 1:9–11)

The Preacher is saying that no matter what we do with our lives, all of us are driven to be exceptional in what we do. But in this quest we will always come up empty. Our name will never be great enough.

Take, for example, the story of television news anchor Brian Williams. He won awards for his coverage of the aftermath of Hurricane Katrina in New Orleans in 2005. Soon afterward he took over for Tom Brokaw as anchor of NBC's flagship program, *Nightly News*. Under his direction as lead anchor, *Nightly News* consistently led all networks as the most-viewed nightly broadcast. Williams signed a lucrative multiyear contract extension near the end of 2014. Then he got caught. Williams was accused of, and gradually admitted to, making up stories on air about near-death battlefield experiences during his reporting on the Iraq War ten years earlier.[7] Before the story broke, he was

---

7. See, for example, "Brian Williams Suspended from NBC for 6 Months without Pay" *New York Times*, February 10, 2015, https://www.nytimes.com/2015/02/11/business /media/brian-williams-suspended-by-nbc-news-for-six-months.html?_r=0.

listed as the twenty-third most trusted person in America. The day after the story broke, he'd fallen more than eight hundred spots, to a range he shared with Willie Robertson of A&E's *Duck Dynasty*.[8]

Why would a man with his accomplishments, his credentials, and his opportunities risk everything to make up stories about himself? His résumé was nearly unmatched already. Why wasn't this enough? Williams's actions show that he knew implicitly what Ecclesiastes claims at the end of the poem in chapter 1: "There is no remembrance of former things, nor will there be any remembrance of later things yet to be among those who come after" (1:11).

The quest to make a name for yourself will always be futile because people won't remember. In our digital age, attention spans are short. We live under a flood of information and a world of options competing for our focus. Given this what-have-you-done-for-me-lately mentality, if you want to be known for your work, you have to keep producing. You have to keep working to stay above the noise. And you'll never have done enough. But the problem is far bigger than our digital age and the challenge of holding the attention of your peers. Even if your work was of such a quality that everyone everywhere knew of and respected you, you will still, one day, be forgotten by "those who come after." As the Preacher observes, things that haven't even happened yet will one day, certainly, be forgotten. No one makes a name for himself in the end.

Pleasure

Maybe you aren't connecting with the Preacher's perspective on work. Maybe for you work seems more like a means to an end.

---

8. See "Brian Williams Loses Lofty Spot on a Trustworthiness Scale," *New York Times*, February 9, 2015, https://www.nytimes.com/2015/02/10/business/media/under-fire-brian-williams-loses-lofty-spot-on-a-trustworthiness-scale.html.

What you want out of life is pleasure. You're only working for the weekend, so to speak.

In chapter 2, the Preacher describes a second experiment in his quest for some sort of gain in life. "I said in my heart, 'Come now, I will test you with pleasure; enjoy yourself.'" He wanted to know "what was good for the children of man to do under heaven during the few days of their life" (Eccles. 2:1, 3). From here the next several verses offer a catalog of all the places he looked for pleasure. He looked to comedy for distraction and leisure (2:2). He tried to cheer himself with wine (2:3). He took up building projects, gardening, and landscape architecture (2:4–6). But he did only what he felt like doing; he had slaves to do whatever he didn't want to do for himself (2:7).

He had herds and flocks greater than any before him in Jerusalem (Eccles. 2:7). He had silver and gold in abundance, and with it status, security, and the ability to buy whatever he wanted (2:8). He had entertainment at his beck and call (2:8). And he had a harem of concubines for basically unlimited, no-strings-attached sex (2:8).

In his quest for pleasure he lived like a god, as if there were no authority over him and no responsibility binding him. It's almost as if he's describing another Eden, a garden paradise of his own making. Only this time there are no rules.[9]

Here's how he summarized his quest: "So I became great and surpassed all who were before me in Jerusalem. . . . And whatever my eyes desired I did not keep from them. I kept my heart from no pleasure, for my heart found pleasure in all my toil, and this was my reward for all my toil" (Eccles. 2:9–10). In his world he never held himself back, no one ever told him no, and no circumstance ever got in his way.

---

9. For this connection to Eden, see Derek Kidner, *The Message of Ecclesiastes* (Downers Grove, IL: InterVarsity Press, 1976), 32.

Perhaps you think you'd be happier if that were true of your life. Have you considered that you may be living his experiment and not know it? The point of the Preacher's elaborate list is to impress you with all he was able to enjoy.[10] He lived a charmed life—the upper 1 percent of his day, and then some. But all the things he lists that made him unusual in what he was able to enjoy—and far more—are available to most people in the Western world.

If you belong to the American middle class, you can get affordable wine and exotic food from all over the world, and you don't have to go to some specialty food store to get them. You can get these things at many corner gas stations. You may not live in a palace like Versailles, surrounded by elaborately designed parks, but you probably live in a house with more space than you need with plenty of parks close at hand. You don't have servants, but chances are you have the money to pay people to do at least some of the work you aren't able or don't want to do. We pay lawyers to represent us. We pay doctors to care for us. We pay professionals to prepare our taxes and, on at least some occasions, chefs to prepare our food. And though the harem of concubines isn't common in the West, the tragic proliferation of internet pornography means that perhaps no society has ever had more opportunities for more people to pursue wide-ranging sexual experiences than does ours.

The Preacher's list begins to sound a bit more like a description of middle-class life, does it not? And we could add to our list a host of opportunities he couldn't have imagined. We have air

---

10. Lists of accomplishments and possessions like this one were common inscriptions for ancient Near Eastern kings. They were meant to celebrate the greatness of the king, to set him apart from what is normal. Of course, in the Preacher's list, the point is that though he's surpassed everyone else, he's ended up in the same place. Choon-Leong Seow has a helpful discussion of the similarities and differences of this list among other ancient examples. He concludes, "Such listings are supposed to show the king to be more successful than the ordinary person and more accomplished than all other kings who preceded him. But Qohelet itemizes the king's many accomplishments only to show that even Solomon, Israel's most glamorous king, is no better off than ordinary people in some ways" (*Ecclesiastes*, The Anchor Yale Bible Commentaries [New Haven, CT: Yale University Press, 1997], 151).

conditioning. We have international travel. We have access to advanced medical care—not just life-saving treatments but drugs to take away discomforts previous generations took for granted as part of life. For entertainment, he had private singers. We have iTunes and online streaming. We have televisions, tablets, and smartphones. He never went to Disney World or Las Vegas or the Metropolitan Museum of Art. We devote a tremendous amount of time and money to the pursuit of pleasure and, for opportunities, our culture takes a back seat to no other time or place.

Because our lives reflect the Preacher's to such an extent, we owe it to ourselves to listen carefully to his conclusion. The results of his experiment were not encouraging: "Then I considered all that my hands had done and the toil I had expended in doing it, and behold, all was vanity and a striving after wind, and there was nothing to be gained under the sun" (Eccles. 2:11). Or, as he put it: "I said . . . of pleasure, 'What use is it?'" (2:2). In the end, pleasure is of no use. This man had everything, and he gained nothing. What has pleasure gained for you? Have you had enough yet?

Wealth

The Preacher's list of pleasures hints at another of the book's major themes—another object of his quest to find something more than vanity and striving after wind. He pursued and obtained great wealth, more, he claimed, than anyone before him in Jerusalem (Eccles. 2:7). And here again, both in what he obtained and in what he concluded, his experience is remarkably modern.

The author could not have imagined the wealth of even the middle class in our culture. To borrow another example from Easterbrook's *Progress Paradox*, consider the mass marketing of high-end watches. Here is what's known as a first-world problem: high-end watches are self-winding, meaning that they draw their energy from the movement of the wrist, so what do you do if you own more than one? If they're not worn, they won't keep accurate time. What can you do if you want to keep your unused watches on time? "What you do in that event is go to the Asprey and Garrard store on Fifth Avenue in NYC and put down $5,700 for a calfskin box in which six electrically powered wrists slowly rotate, winding your self-winding high-end watches."[11]

The Preacher never envisioned a $6,000 box to wind his unworn watches, much less one sold for $200 by Brookstone aimed at middle-class owners of multiple high-end watches. But his assessment of his own wealth predicts precisely our experience with the futility of money. No matter how much you have, when you love your wealth, you will never have enough. "He who loves money will not be satisfied with money, nor he who loves wealth with his income; this also is vanity" (Eccles. 5:10). The more you have, the more you will want. All wealth is vanity—empty, meaningless, nothing.

I wonder: have you ever felt as if you had everything you wanted? Sure, there is some happiness that can come with more money and with what you can buy with more money. That rush of happiness lies behind so many of our purchases. It's difficult to put that feeling into words—why our whole world can look different, for a moment, after the purchase of a new car, a new house, even a new outfit or a new gadget. It is as if these things make us feel new. They promise a new beginning of sorts, a chance to rally ourselves and overcome what we don't like about our lives. It almost feels as if things will be different if I'm wearing these new shoes or wielding this new iPhone. Retail therapy isn't just a cliché. There's something to it, for a moment at least. The problem is that this happiness never lasts. We are never truly satisfied with what we have.

---

11. Easterbrook, *Progress Paradox*, 125–26.

Why? In Ecclesiastes 5:11 the Preacher offers an example. "When goods increase, they increase who eat them, and what advantage has their owner but to see them with his eyes?" He doesn't elaborate his point, but I believe it's clear enough. Experience shows that your perceived needs will always rise to meet your resources. Consumption always keeps pace with stock, so you never feel like you've arrived. There's no advantage to the owner but seeing what he has raised or accumulated—he finds no happiness or joy in what he has.

Have you ever felt like you had more than enough? Maybe your income today is significantly greater than it was ten years ago. Maybe if you'd imagined then what you have today, you wouldn't have known how to spend it all. But if your experience is anything like mine, you've found that as your income has grown, so have expected costs. You spend more than you once did on childcare, on utilities, on car payments. Perhaps you have a larger mortgage on your home and pay for insurance on everything you own. What you prefer to eat now costs more than when your tastes were simpler or less refined. Where you eat out, where you go on vacation and for how long, and so many other things rise up to meet the resources that you have. Or, in the words of the Preacher, when goods increase they increase who eat them, and the one who loves wealth is never wealthy enough. Wealth is futile.

Explaining Futility through Death

Bursting Our Bubbles

The Preacher's perspective is remarkably modern. Things keep getting better; we keep feeling worse. No matter what we accomplish or how much we're able to enjoy or how much we acquire, still we feel like we're striving after wind. We never really gain anything. The Preacher's *experience* sounds exactly like ours. But Ecclesiastes offers an *explanation* for futility that has mostly faded out of view in our time and place. Everything is meaningless because everyone dies.

David Gibson describes death in Ecclesiastes as the pin that bursts every bubble we might use to shield ourselves from the truth.[12] Think of work or money or pleasure as balloons. We fill them with our time and our energy and our hope. For a while we watch them expand. From the outside they look to gain mass and, you might even assume, weight. But inside it's only vapor. Death is the needle that shows the truth.

Consider work. Why is it that no matter what I accomplish or how successful I become, I never feel like I've done enough? Because I'm going to die:

> There is no remembrance of former things,
>> nor will there be any remembrance
> of later things yet to be
>> among those who come after. (Eccles. 1:11)

> I hated all my toil in which I toil under the sun, seeing that I must leave it to the man who will come after me. (Eccles. 2:18)

> What has a man from all the toil and striving of heart with which he toils beneath the sun? For all his days are full of sorrow, and his work is a vexation. Even in the night his heart does not rest. This also is vanity. (Eccles. 2:22–23)

What we gain from work is stress, vexation, and sleepless nights. Why? We want our lives to make a mark. We want to accomplish things that matter. We want to do something that will last. We keep running, keep pressing, like hamsters on their wheels—stressed out to no good end. Because nothing we do can change the fact that we will die, and eventually the best we

---

12. David Gibson, *Destiny: Learning to Live by Preparing to Die* (Leicester, UK: Inter-Varsity Press, 2016), 23.

accomplish will collapse like an elaborate sandcastle in the rising tide.[13] Or as Julian Barnes puts it, at best our work is like graffiti on the cell wall of the condemned prisoner. We're etching into the stones, "I was here."[14] But even if our work survives for a time in someone's memory, "I was here" is just another way of saying "I'm not here now."

The same culprit lies behind our experience of wealth. Why is it that every time I reach my financial goals or purchase what I thought I wanted, I find myself wanting more? Because I'm going to die. Speaking of a rich man, the Preacher warns, "As he came from his mother's womb he shall go again, naked as he came, and shall take nothing for his toil that he may carry away in his hand. This also is a grievous evil: just as he came, so shall he go, and what gain is there to him who toils for the wind?" (Eccles. 5:15–16).

You never feel like you have enough wealth because you can't take any of it with you. Death is certain. That means no matter how much you own, you have nothing.

Every now and then I check out an estate sale in our city, typically when the advertiser mentions lots of books. Browsing around one of these sales is an interesting experience, even somewhat bizarre. There's an intimacy to it, for one thing. You're in someone else's home. You're rifling through things that once belonged to someone else. You know that every piece must have a backstory. One of these novels was her favorite. One of those chairs was the place he sat every night before bed. Did someone give him this watch as a birthday present? Did she buy that dress for some special occasion?

In an estate sale you're browsing through someone else's carefully curated life, usually after she's died. The Preacher is telling us to think of all our wealth and all it's bought for us not from the

13. I owe this image to Gibson, *Destiny*, 6.
14. Julian Barnes, *Nothing to Be Frightened Of* (New York: Vintage, 2009), 201.

perspective of the immediate thrill but from the perspective of our estate sales. For all our time and attention, no matter how carefully we curate our stuff or how much we might enjoy ourselves along the way, we're all merely stocking and staging someone else's opportunity for bargain prices.

The Problem Is the Destination

Your trouble with futility has little to do with what you haven't yet experienced, or haven't yet accomplished, or haven't yet acquired. The problem is not that you haven't arrived. The problem is where you're going. That is the crucial insight we must gain from Ecclesiastes.

> The wise person has his eyes in his head, but the fool walks in darkness. And yet I perceived that the same event happens to all of them. Then I said in my heart, "What happens to the fool will happen to me also. Why then have I been so very wise?" And I said in my heart that this also is vanity. For of the wise as of the fool there is no enduring remembrance, seeing that in the days to come all will have been long forgotten. How the wise dies just like the fool! So I hated life, because what is done under the sun was grievous to me, for all is vanity and a striving after wind. (Eccles. 2:14–17)

> I said in my heart with regard to the children of man that God is testing them that they may see that they themselves are but beasts. For what happens to the children of man and what happens to the beasts is the same; as one dies, so dies the other. They all have the same breath, and man has no advantage over the beasts, for all is vanity. All go to one place. All are from the dust, and to dust all return. (Eccles. 3:18–20)

Death has an unmatched ability to expose the flimsiness of the things we believe give substance to our lives. To borrow an image from Camus, death exposes the things we love and trust with our lives as nothing more than set pieces on a stage.[15] From a distance, at a glance, that may look like a deep-rooted tree or a solid load-bearing wall. But walk off set, and you see any substance is an illusion—an appearance of strength that only stands so long as it's propped up. Death is the push of a finger or the gust of wind that topples them over one by one.

When you experience futility, you're experiencing the power of death to topple what you thought to be substantive and secure. Ecclesiastes was written to help you learn what the Preacher learned, and sooner rather than later. It's specifically aimed at the young, those whose lives are mostly out in front of them, because when we're young, we're most susceptible to self-deception. We tend to live heavily invested in what tomorrow will bring. We think of our lives like ladders we're climbing rung by rung. Finish school. Pay off loans. Find a spouse and have some kids. Buy a home. Then buy a better one. Get tenure. Make partner. These goals seem so real, so substantive and worthwhile. They especially seem substantive and worthwhile before you reach them. When so much of what you want from life is still out in front of you, it's difficult to see for yourself what the Preacher had to learn the hard way. The truth is, life isn't a ladder at all. It's more like an ice-covered mountain down which you've been slipping and sliding since the day you were born.

If this perspective on life still sounds abstract or unconvincing, try this thought experiment. Think of something you desperately want. Maybe it is something you've been working toward for years: completed dissertation, partnership at your law firm, successful launch of your own business. Maybe it's something that will set up your career for years to come: a major grant award

---

15. Albert Camus, "The Myth of Sisyphus," trans. Justin O'Brien, in *The Plague, the Fall, Exile and the Kingdom, and Selected Essays* (New York: Knopf, 2004), 502–3.

for your research, or some such. Maybe it's a basic building block to your life: finding a spouse or having children or settling down in a wonderful city. Maybe it's a purchase you've been wishing or even saving for: a new house or a fishing boat or whatever makes sense for you. Think of some unfulfilled ambition that's with you every day, filling your thoughts, taking your time, moving your affections. What is that for you?

Now imagine one day you get what you've wanted. There's immediate relief and excitement. You pass on the good news to all your friends. You make plans to celebrate. Later that same day you have a follow-up appointment with your doctor to receive some test results. You went in a week earlier complaining of back pain and persistent headaches. Nothing terribly unusual, just uncomfortable and annoying. Now your doctor says he has bad news. He begins to use words like "stage 4," "inoperable," and "terminal." Imagine that on that single day, you learn that you have achieved what you've been longing for, and you have only six months to live. Be honest: Which piece of news is likely to define your day?

Surgeon Paul Kalanithi faced almost this exact dilemma. He tells his own story beautifully in his memoir *When Breath Becomes Air*, published in 2015 shortly after he died of cancer. Kalanithi had endured nearly two decades of wildly successful training at some of the world's finest institutions. A year away from finishing his surgery fellowship he had already received a range of offers of prestigious jobs perfectly tailored to his interests. Everything he had worked so hard and so well to achieve was nearly within his reach, when he learned that he had an advanced and vicious form of cancer.

Near the end of the book, he describes the disorienting effect of death on a life always lived with an eye to the future. "Medical training is relentlessly future-oriented, all about delayed gratification; you're always thinking about what you'll be doing five years down the line." It's natural, in other words, to think of the future as a ladder you're climbing. But death, when honestly confronted, reframes everything: "Most ambitions are either achieved or abandoned; either way, they belong to the past. The future, instead of the ladder toward the goals of life, flattens out into a perpetual present. Money, status, all the vanities the preacher of Ecclesiastes described hold so little interest: a chasing after wind, indeed."[16]

Kalanithi's story has a gripping power because it is so tragic and unexpected. It captivates at least in part because it seems exceptional to us. But Kalanithi echoes the warning of Ecclesiastes: there is nothing exceptional about the substance of his story. Everyone's diagnosis is terminal. That fact, acknowledged or not, has a devastating effect on the meaning of what matters to us. You can try to dodge the weight of futility by assuming fulfillment will come when you reach your goals. You can convince yourself you're dissatisfied only because you haven't finished climbing the ladder. You can believe the key to happiness is what you haven't yet reached. Tomorrow can seem like your greatest friend. Tomorrow holds your highest hopes. But in fact, if we limit our view to life "under the sun," tomorrow is not a friend. It is your great enemy. Tomorrow is when you die.[17]

Futility, Death, and Idolatry

To acknowledge the truth about death is to confront haunting questions about life under the sun. If all there is to life is swallowed up by the nothingness of death, what does it even mean to make the most of your life? Or, in the Preacher's terms, is there any gain in my life that death won't empty out? At root it is a fun-

---

16. Paul Kalanithi, *When Breath Becomes Air* (New York: Random House, 2016), 197–98.
17. I owe this observation on tomorrow to Albert Camus, "The Myth of Sisyphus," 503.

damentally religious question: What can deliver me from death? What can overcome death's power? Where can I look for hope and purpose?

Ernest Becker argues that behind our attempts to make a mark lies "the ache of cosmic specialness": "The hope and belief is that the things that man creates in society are of lasting worth and meaning, that they outlive or outshine death and decay, that man and his products count." In everything we do, Becker argues, we're driven by "a hopeful belief and protest that science, money and goods make man count for more than any other animal. In this sense everything that man does is religious and heroic, and yet in danger of being fictitious and fallible."[18]

In danger of being fictitious and fallible—from the Preacher's perspective, that's putting it mildly. More like *guaranteed* to be fictitious and fallible, or, to stick to our category, futile. Futility is a relative term. To describe something as futile is to say it is not useful *for* some specific purpose. Behind our experience of life's futility is the unrecognized and fruitless attempt to overcome death. We experience futility in work or pleasure or wealth or whatever else when these things are not able to do what we're asking them to do. We're asking them to protect us from death—to give our lives meaning that death won't erase. And for this purpose, they are futile. We're building walls and roofs out of tissue paper and asking them to give us shelter from the rain.[19]

When we experience futility, we taste the power of death to expose the false gods we've set up in our lives—gods that we've designed for ourselves and asked to deliver us. We make gods of work or money or relationships or any number of good but created things when we love them or trust them or obey *them,*

---

18. Ernest Becker, *The Denial of Death* (New York: Free Press, 1973), 4–5.
19. I owe the image of tissue paper in a rainstorm to Jonathan Franzen, *The Corrections* (New York: Farrar, Straus and Giroux, 2001), 308.

instead of the God who made them and us.[20] Ecclesiastes exposes another reason behind why we look to these things for meaning or significance or justification. We're looking to them to protect us from death.

Sociologist Peter Berger has argued that we should view all religions as banners to which people rally in the battle against death. "The power of religion depends, in the last resort, upon the credibility of the banners it puts in the hands of men as they stand before death, or more accurately, as they walk, inevitably, toward it."[21] In other words, death is the great standard of evaluation. The goal of religious activity and religious hope is meaning in light of death. And the way to judge whether a religion is dependable or futile is to consider how it confronts the power of death.

Berger had in mind more traditional, organized religions, but the same principle holds true in more secular contexts like ours. We may be less prone to trust institutions, sign off on belief statements, and go through all the rituals than previous generations. But that doesn't mean we're any less religious. It doesn't mean we're any less hungry for any source of deliverance from the power of death. We're just not as self-aware as others have been.

These gods of our making have nothing we don't provide for ourselves. How could they have power to overcome what we are powerless to face on our own?

When we look to work or pleasure or money for protection, we place ourselves in the helpless position of Isaiah's comical

---

20. In recent years, authors like David Powlison and Tim Keller have helped us recognize the old truth that gods come in all shapes and sizes. See David Powlison, "Idols of the Heart and 'Vanity Fair,'" *Journal of Biblical Counseling*, 13, no. 2 (Winter 1995): 35–50; Tim Keller, *Counterfeit Gods: The Empty Promises of Money, Sex, and Power, and the Only Hope That Matters* (New York: Dutton, 2009).

21. Peter Berger, *The Sacred Canopy: Elements of a Sociological Theory of Religion* (New York: Random House, 1967), 51. See also chapter 3, "The Problem of Theodicy."

craftsman. Isaiah 44 gives one of the Bible's most devastating critiques of the futility of idolatry. The account begins with a pronouncement that echoes the Preacher's language of vanity: "All who fashion idols are nothing, and the things they delight in do not profit" (Isa. 44:9). There it is: no profit. Where is the gain? The prophet's focus is the uselessness or futility of idols. What follows reads like a cross between a courtroom scene and a satirical short story.

Isaiah takes us into a workshop of sorts for a firsthand look at idol-making in rewind. First we see an ironsmith fashioning the metal, presumably as a cover for the god. "The ironsmith takes a cutting tool and works it over the coals. He fashions it with hammers and works it with his strong arm" (Isa. 44:12).

Moving back one step in the process, we see the carpenter working with a block of wood, thinking through shape and design. What should this god look like? What design makes sense? He opts for the best he can imagine: himself. "He shapes it into the figure of a man, with the beauty of a man, to dwell in a house" (Isa. 44:13).

Then we're taken back to material selection: "He cuts down cedars, or he chooses a cypress tree or an oak and lets it grow strong among the trees of the forest. He plants a cedar and the rain nourishes it" (v. 14). Like the craftsman himself, all of his materials belong to this world and depend on its resources to survive.

One final step exposes the ridiculous, arbitrary trust we place in gods we make for ourselves. The craftsman cuts down his selected tree. He saws the tree in two. Then this: "Half of it he burns in the fire. Over the half he eats meat; he roasts it and is satisfied. Also he warms himself and says, 'Aha, I am warm, I have seen the fire!' And the rest of it he makes into a god, his idol, and falls down to it and worships it. He prays to it and says, 'Deliver me, for you are my god!'" (Isa. 44:16–17).

The comedy is unmistakable. It's easy to assume we would never worship or rely on something we made for ourselves. We know a piece of wood, no matter how well-carved, has no power to deliver us. It's good in itself. Useful for warmth, for food, for some sort of shelter. But turning to a block of wood for deliverance is arbitrary and useless. We know that. We're enlightened now.

But the allure of idolatry is timeless. A god of our making serves our ends and does our bidding. A god of our making testifies to our skill, our craftsmanship, our ingenuity, our glory. But that sword is double-edged. Our idols have no power beyond what we give them. They don't hear us when we call out for deliverance. When we look to them for help, they do not look back. Eventually, they die with us.

I have never seen Isaiah's point more clearly than when I watched the decline and death of my maternal grandfather. He was one of the most accomplished and well-regarded men I have known. He built a thriving career as a business executive, served for a time in state government, and worked off and on for years developing the business community of the small town where he lived. So far as I know, he was loved and respected by most of those who knew him. He enjoyed some measure of power, and he had a status many men aspire to reach. He also had emphysema for nearly thirty years.

I remember when his health became too great a problem for him to continue working full-time. He had to leave the business world in which he thrived, but he still wanted to work. I remember him taking a succession of part-time jobs, one at a call center and others at a couple of different shoe stores. Even as a child I wondered what that must be like—to have been on the staff of the state governor and, now, to be pulling different sizes for complaining, entitled teenagers in the market for new Nikes.

Then I remember when he and my grandmother moved to the town where I grew up, to be closer to family. It is a smaller town than where he moved from, but no one knew him there. I remember that he sought out volunteer work at the local chamber of commerce. They never called him back. He had been a key member of the governor's staff; now he couldn't work for free in this small town.

A few years later, after his health had sharply declined, a hospice company took charge of his care. They placed him in a hospital bed, one of those metal ones with the droppable railing. This bed needed to be on the ground floor of his home to make things accessible, so they placed the bed in my grandfather's office. The bed sat next to a wall that was covered, nearly floor to ceiling, by plaques given to recognize his accomplishments and his service to the community. My grandfather died in that bed, underneath those monuments to a life more celebrated than most.

A year or so after his death, there was some question about what to do with all the plaques. In the end, my family decided to give them to a neighbor with a woodworking hobby, thinking he could make use of the wood in one of his projects. I felt a pang of surprise and regret when I first heard the news. Not that it was the wrong decision. I knew it made good sense. But it felt like what was left of my grandfather's life—whatever gain he had—was about to become raw material in an amateur woodshop. It felt like a profane use of sacred objects. But in reality, in Isaiah's terms, those plaques were far better suited to a tinker's shop or a cooking fire than to deliver my grandfather from death.

Death exposes our idols for what they are: false gods with no power to save. At best, anything we accomplish, anything we enjoy, anything we acquire amounts to nothing more than roofs and walls made of tissue paper. They will never protect us from the storm that's coming. And that's why everything feels futile, meaningless. That's what Ecclesiastes has shown us.

Ecclesiastes is also a warning: Don't wait until the end of your life to test the character of what you're trusting. You're facing death now just as surely as you will be in forty or sixty years. And in your experience of futility the weakness of your protection is already showing.

Overcoming Futility with Purpose

One writer has called Ecclesiastes "the most striking messianic prophecy the Old Testament has to offer."[22] I believe he's right. The book is relentlessly bleak. At points the Preacher looks beyond the sun to the realm of the Creator, calling his readers to enjoy what God has given while they can. But for the most part he stays on point, and he finishes where he began: "Vanity of vanities, says the Preacher; all is vanity" (Eccles. 12:8). Ecclesiastes is not messianic in the way of Isaiah. There are no promises of deliverance to come, no expectation that someone will one day break into the monotonous cycle of vanity and bring something new. But Ecclesiastes is messianic in its own way: it sets the context in which the resurrection of Jesus makes sense. It prepares us to see why everything is vain if Jesus is not alive. So, by contrast, it helps us see how everything matters if Jesus is alive.

This vanity seems to be in the background of Paul's thinking in 1 Corinthians 15, a chapter fully devoted to defending the necessity and revealing the beauty of Jesus's resurrection. I want to conclude this reflection on futility by following Paul's argument about what Jesus has done to transform what is possible for us.

---

22. H. W. Hertzberg, *Der Prediger*, cited by Kidner, *The Wisdom of Proverbs, Job and Ecclesiastes*, 114.

If Jesus Is Not Raised, Our Faith Is as Vain as Everything Else

Paul seems to be responding to some in Corinth who did not understand the importance of resurrection or, perhaps, did not believe it was possible. He reminds them what he told them at the first, what was handed down to him too: that Christ died, he was buried, and on the third day he was raised. He reminds them of the evidence: the apostles saw him, five hundred brothers saw him at once, and Paul saw him too. But Paul goes one step further. It is not just that this is what has been handed down as true. It is not just part of the tradition. The point is that it *must be true* or Christianity itself is pointless: "If Christ has not been raised, then our preaching is in vain and your faith is in vain" (1 Cor. 15:14).

The Greek word Paul uses for "vain" has a similar range of meaning to the Hebrew word that is Ecclesiastes' catchphrase.[23] Knowing Paul was a rigorous, well-trained scholar of the Hebrew Bible, it is not difficult to imagine that he has the message of Ecclesiastes in mind as he reflects on the nonnegotiable importance of Jesus's resurrection. He is telling the Corinthians that if Jesus is not alive again, then their faith is just as vain as everything else. It's as vain as pleasure, money, or work. It's just another set piece propped up on stage. Another wall of tissue paper that will only dissolve in the storm. Another piece of wood we have arbitrarily decided to worship rather than to burn. If Christ isn't raised—if he couldn't face death and overcome it—then he is vain, and our faith in him is vain, and our lives remain pitiable, foolish, and empty. "And if Christ has not been raised, your faith is futile and you are

---

23. The Greek word is *kenos*, which means "empty." Used figuratively, it's meaning should sound familiar by this point: "without result, without profit, without effect, without reaching its goal" (W. Bauer, F. W. Danker, W. F. Arndt, and F. W. Gingrich, *A Greek-English Lexicon of the New Testament and Other Early Christian Literature*, 2nd ed.(Chicago: University of Chicago Press, 1979), 427.

still in your sins. Then those also who have fallen asleep in Christ have perished. If in Christ we have hope in this life only, we are of all people most to be pitied" (1 Cor. 15:17–19).

In these verses Paul essentially accepts Peter Berger's terms. Remember how Berger condensed the purpose of religion: "The power of religion depends, in the last resort, upon the credibility of the banners it puts in the hands of men as they stand before death, or more accurately, as they walk, inevitably, toward it." Paul echoes—really, foreshadows—that assessment here in 1 Corinthians 15. If Christ is not raised, then he can't raise us. If he can't raise us? "If we have hope in this life only"? If what's "under the sun" is all there is? Then Paul's life is striving after wind. It is pointless and empty. All his sacrifices are wasted, and he deserves pity. The perspective of Ecclesiastes has prepared Paul for desperate dependence on the promise of resurrection. It is resurrection or vanity.

But in Fact Christ Has Been Raised

This desperation sets the stage for what comes next: "But in fact Christ has been raised from the dead, the firstfruits of those who have fallen asleep" (1 Cor. 15:20). In fact our faith is not futile but powerfully effective. Christ didn't try to evade death by pleasurable self-medication. He didn't try to rise above death by a résumé of accomplishments others would remember when he was gone. He faced death head-on. He took the fight to death's territory, went into its very depths, and emerged victorious once and for all. And he did this not for himself only, but as a firstfruits of what is to come. In Paul's words: "As by a man came death, by a man has come also the resurrection of the dead. For as in Adam all die, so also in Christ shall all be made alive" (15:21–22).

Paul is announcing that Christ has made our enemy his enemy. Death is no longer our battle to fight. "Then comes the end, when he delivers the kingdom to God the Father after destroying every rule and every authority and power. For he must reign until he has put all his enemies under his feet. The last enemy to be destroyed is death" (1 Cor. 15:24–26). The fact of Christ's resurrection shows that this sequence is set in motion, and nothing can stop its force. It depends on us for nothing. Christ does it all. He has made death his final enemy, and he has crushed its power.

And Since Christ Has Been Raised . . .

Now we're ready to see how Paul applies Jesus to our experience of futility. Remember the roots of futility we've unearthed: the things that matter to us in life feel futile because they matter too much—because we look to them for meaning that death won't erase, and they can't deliver. As foundations for lives of substance, our work, our money, our pleasure-seeking will always remain empty. We trust them in vain. Paul has argued the same test applies to Jesus—if he can't survive the threat of death, our faith in him is futile and empty too. We may find his talk on loving one another inspiring or sentimental. We may find him a helpful guru for insight on making the most of the time we have. We may admire him as a model of a man who stood by his convictions to the end. But if he is reduced to a set of teachings to understand or an example to follow, our faith in him is vain. He is no deliverer. We are left to face death on our own. We're left to medicate our hearts, chasing the next pleasure. We'll keep trying to fill our lives with stuff, not recognizing that the more we pour in, the more drains out through a hole in the bottom of the glass. Every glass ends up empty. And we'll keep working to justify our lives with some monument others will envy and, maybe, even remember for a while after we're gone. But experience shows that death crushes any defense we may raise.

But what if Christ has already defeated our enemy for us? What if death is not our enemy to fight? What if the purpose of our lives is no longer aimed at overcoming the grave? What is our purpose then? What is the use of the things that matter to us in life?

Let's take just one example, our work. If Christ has conquered death for me, accomplishing what I have uselessly asked my work to do, how does his work change the way I pursue mine right now? This is exactly where Paul applies his long argument about the importance of resurrection. In the final verse of 1 Corinthians 15, Paul draws a conclusion made all the sweeter by the bitterness of Ecclesiastes: "Therefore, my beloved brothers, be steadfast, immovable, always abounding in the work of the Lord, knowing that in the Lord your labor is not in vain" (15:58).

Your labor is not in vain. Not anymore. Not when death isn't your problem to overcome. Your work matters now. It has substance and meaning. It is something, not nothing. It has purpose. But notice that Paul's encouragement is sharply specific. It is only in the Lord that your labor is not in vain. What does it mean to pursue our work "in the Lord"? How does that yield work that matters? The promise of meaningful work in the Lord is both a call to repent and also a call to believe.

First, we must repent of any work not done in the Lord. We must give up on any work we might do to establish names for ourselves. That work has nothing to do with Jesus. It aims at an identity separate from him. And all such work dies with us.

This means you have to stop fantasizing about how badly your high school friends will envy you at the fifteen- or twenty-year reunion. You have to stop using benchmark birthdays to measure how well you're doing at twenty-five, then thirty, then forty and fifty. More often than not, when we stop to size ourselves up against our goals or what others have accomplished, we're looking for self-justification. We're assuming we're climbing a ladder, and we're checking to see how far we've climbed. We're pretending that we're not skidding down that ice-covered mountain. We're working as if it's possible to build a name for ourselves outside of Jesus. And we're working as if his work for us isn't already perfect and complete.

Anytime we recognize that our identities are caught up in what we accomplish, we need to remember the words of the Preacher. We should think of our work as the etchings of a prisoner on his cell wall, scratching out "I was here" in the hope that someone might someday read it. We must learn to bow out of that losing game now, while we can.

When death-awareness leads us to quick and regular repentance, our work provides daily opportunities to press deeper into the rest that Jesus came to offer us. Into the monotony of generations that rise and fall, come and go, here for a moment and then forgotten, something new has happened. A light has dawned, and the darkness of Ecclesiastes is here to help us see it. The God who made us has come to us, entered the darkness we have chosen for ourselves, absorbed the just punishment for our sin in his death, and made new life possible in his resurrection.

Now this God tells us stop trying to defeat death by our work, because he has defeated death by his work. This promise adds some concreteness to Jesus's words in Matthew 11: "Come to me, all who labor and are heavy laden, and I will give you rest. Take my yoke upon you, and learn from me, for I am gentle and lowly in heart, and you will find rest for your souls. For my yoke is easy, and my burden is light" (v. 28). Ironically, our work in the Lord is itself an opportunity for deep and blessed rest. But it's a rest we enter only through repentance.

Second, we must believe that no work is pointless if it's done in the Lord. Work in the Lord identifies with him and comes motivated by what he's done.

Believing this about our work will remain a challenge, of course, for as long as we remain under the sun. For now we will continue to be frustrated and disappointed and exhausted and prideful in our work. Sometimes what we're doing will seem pointless. Sometimes what we're doing won't seem nearly as effective or compelling as what someone else is doing. We will still have tasks we perform on repeat—thankless, unseen, feeling like we accomplish nothing.

And there is some truth in what we feel. Our work on its own will not stand the test of time. If that's what we want from our work, it will never be successful, and it will never be finished.

But when we're in Christ, when we feel frustrated or disappointed by work that isn't what we wanted it to be, or when we feel worn down by work that is monotonous or uninspiring, our experience becomes an opportunity to remember the truth about Jesus's work and to refocus what we're doing in our work. We work in Christ. For his name, not ours. Pursuing his agenda, not ours. "So, whether you eat or drink, or whatever you do, do all to the glory of God" (1 Cor. 10:31).

Through this calling our work takes on a new purpose that is always attainable, no matter the task. Are you stuck in a cubicle manipulating spreadsheets all day every day? Praise God you get to reflect the glory of the One who put every star in its place, marked off the oceans, and ordered every species.

Are your days are filled with tasks that never move anywhere and never get finished? Are there always more reports to file or more exams to grade or more dishes to wash or more meals to prepare? Thank Jesus that his work is finished. That means your work doesn't have to be finished to be useful, or even satisfying. With each new day and each new task you have an opportunity to reflect the life and love of the One who lived and died and rose for you. Your Lord took up the towel and washed the feet of his disciples. He calls his servants to do as he has done, which means he is pleased when you serve others in his name. No work that pleases him will ever be in vain.

As a defense against death, our work is futile. But when we embrace the victory of Jesus, accepting that death is not our enemy to destroy, we can finally embrace what has been our chief end all along: to glorify God and enjoy him forever.

4

The Problem of Loss and the Promise of Eternal Life

I don't remember when it first hit me, but now I notice it every year. Since long before we had kids, my family has taken an annual trip to the white sandy beaches near where my wife and I grew up. As spring begins to drift into summer, we begin to live for this trip. Each year, when the day finally arrives, we pull our heavy-laden vehicle into the drop-off lane at the entrance to the condominium complex. We go inside to grab a cart for all the luggage. We load up the cart and head for the elevators. Inevitably, at some point during this process, we pass by someone else pushing a luggage cart. Only this person is coming off the elevator. They're heading out to their car, away from their condo. Their vacation in paradise is over. I notice this, every year, and I realize that soon enough we'll be packing back up too. As soon as I'm there, ready to enjoy sun-filled days in one of my favorite places on earth, I'm thinking about leaving. It nags at me all week.

I suppose this annual experience is at least one of the reasons I connect so deeply with Virginia Woolf's novel *To the Lighthouse*.

It has become one of my favorite novels, but I wouldn't call it a pleasant read. In many ways its setting, characters, and plot are commonplace, even mundane, but it's a haunting book. Woolf frames her story around the experience of a vacation, longed for and beloved, that must eventually come to an end.[1] And through the story we get a taste of what all of us must discover over time: our childhood experience of holidays that don't last long enough turns out to be a pretty good metaphor for all of life.

The book begins with the vibrant Ramsay family on an extended holiday by the sea. Mr. and Mrs. Ramsay are surrounded by all of their children and even many of their friends, filling their summer home and its grounds with life and adventure and joy and love. The kids pass their time playing on the beach or exploring the grounds. The adults are lounging or reading or painting or gardening or strolling through the beautiful scenery, always together. And in the evenings their dinner table is always full—full of wonderful food, of vibrant conversation, of people who love one another celebrating the joy of being together.

The middle section of the book changes tone completely. It doesn't really narrate any events. It's a lyrical, almost mystical diversion on the ravaging of time and death. Along the way, it becomes clear that the family is not taking summer vacations anymore. Life has intervened. The house that had been so full of joy sits empty for years, unused and decaying.

The final section of the book returns to the summer home with what's left of the family and their friends. What's been lost is terribly obvious. One of the sons was killed in war. The mother had been the joyful and nurturing center of the family;

---

1. Virginia Woolf, *To the Lighthouse* (1927; New York: Harcourt Brace and Company, 1989).

now she, too, has died. The remaining children have lost their innocence and wonder. In the first section the kids are desperate for a boat ride to an old lighthouse nearby. The father is too occupied with his own work to take them. In the final section it's the father who is desperate to go. He drags his reluctant teenagers behind him, grasping for some taste of what they'd had before, dying slowly to the lost world he had been too busy to fully enjoy.

Woolf's beautiful, sad story points the way to a critical insight. Good things never last. Time and death turn sweet seasons of life into painful memories of what's been lost.

This world is a marvelous place. We enjoy the beauty of its landscapes, its music, its arts and cultures. And, above all, we enjoy its people—our spouses and children, our parents and grandparents, our brothers and sisters and friends and neighbors. Yet it is precisely our love of the good things in life that gives death much of its power over us. Under death's shadow, time and decay reach as far as our love. And their grip on the things we love is stronger than ours.

One of my goals in this book is to help us recognize the shadow of death in places we may not have seen it before. Death is a biological event—the end of the heart's beating, the lungs' breathing, and the brain's processing—but it is also far more. There's no confining death to the moment at which your life ends. Its effects are everywhere. Death is not so much an event as a process with a final culmination—a siphoning process that separates us from what we love so that, in the end, everyone loses everything. But when we recognize this truth, when we acknowledge it and don't shrink back from it, we join the path to deeper, fuller joy in the promise of a deathless world where what we love won't ever pass away, a world promised to us by the one who is the Resurrection and the Life.

The Many Faces of Death: Everyone Loses Everything

Philosopher Luc Ferry says the driving force behind the study of philosophy is our need to cope with what he calls death's "many different faces." How do we live well in a world where nothing lasts and nothing returns? To understand what Ferry means and why this question is so important, we need to recognize two problems everyone faces that, put together, make for a devastating effect on our lives. These are the problems of impermanence and irreversibility.[2]

Framing the Problem: Impermanence
Meets Irreversibility

The problem of impermanence is simple: with time, everything changes and nothing lasts. Impermanence shows itself all around us, once we've learned to see it. It's in every delicious meal that comes down to a last bite. It's in every great book that comes to its last page and every great show that comes to a final episode. We see it in the changing of every season and in the coming and going of every holiday. Everything good is temporary.

On its own, impermanence is not all bad. The changing of the seasons and the cycle of holidays adds freshness and variety to our lives. If Christmas lasted a year rather than a day or a month, it wouldn't seem so special. We may even grow bored. Part of what gives football season its intensity is the fact that it lasts only three or four months. And we fans take what each season brings knowing that there's always next year.

But what if there weren't always next year? Impermanence takes its full toll when combined with another of death's many faces: irreversibility. Ferry describes death as "that which will not return; that which belongs irreversibly to time past, which we

2. For Ferry's helpful framing of these problems and how they relate to the goals of philosophy, see his *A Brief History of Thought: A Philosophical Guide to Living* (New York: Harper, 2011), 4–10.

have no hope of ever recovering."[3] Time moves in only one direction. That means some good, impermanent things come into our lives, pass out of our lives, and never come back again. Impermanence wed to irreversibility creates the pain of irretrievable loss. This, as Ferry puts it, is "death at the heart of life."[4]

C. S. Lewis captures this pain in a heartbreaking passage of his *A Grief Observed*. The book is an honest and powerful attempt to make sense of the death of his wife, Joy, to cancer. Lewis complains of well-meaning comforters who assure him his wife is in a better place, that her life continues on in God's presence. In his pain, he feels that such comfort misses the point entirely:

> You tell me, "She goes on." But my heart and body are crying out, come back, come back.... But I know this is impossible. I know that the thing I want is exactly the thing I can never get. The old life, the jokes, the drinks, the arguments, the lovemaking, the tiny, heartbreaking commonplace. On any view whatever, to say "H. is dead," is to say "All that is gone." It is a part of the past. And the past is the past and that is what time means, and time itself is one more name for death.[5]

"Time itself is one more name for death." Do you see what Lewis means? Death is so much more than the end of biological life. It isn't a problem you can put off until your final years. Death spreads its poison through everything we enjoy because nothing we enjoy is ours to keep. Time passes, things change, and eventually everyone loses everything they love.

Recognizing the Problem: How to Pay Attention

The problem of loss is a philosophical problem, but not the sort of mind-bending intellectual knot we might normally associate

---

3. Ferry, *Brief History of Thought*, 5.

4. Ferry, *Brief History of Thought*, 7.

5. C. S. Lewis, *A Grief Observed* (1961; New York: Bantam, 1976), 27–28.

with philosophy. It's rather a problem to be experienced in the life of every person past, present, and future. Recognizing the pervasiveness of loss, the truth that time means death, is part of living an honest life in the world as it is, not as we wish it were. In other words, it's foolish of us to think of loss as something exceptional or unexpected. Loss is universal, not exceptional. It's guaranteed, not unexpected. Every relationship is lost to time. So is every penny of everyone's wealth, and ultimately so is every life. Loss isn't surprising. It is basic to the course of every life.

But the younger you are, the harder it is to experience the true weight of this problem. When you're young, it's almost impossible to see that what your life feels like now won't last forever. It's all you've known. There's no standard for comparison. It doesn't matter how many times you're told that time flies, or how many times you're warned by someone older to enjoy what you have while it lasts. It's natural to feel like what you love will go on forever.

If anything, the future promises more gain, not loss. You tend to view your life as a kind of savings account. With each passing year, you're adding new assets, watching the number continue to grow. You're expanding your mind through education. You're getting better at your job. You're developing new hobbies or handy skills. You're forming new and meaningful relationships, or deepening the relationships you already have. Overall, it feels like you're stockpiling things you love about life. So you focus on what you don't have yet and doing what's necessary to get it, not on the prospect of losing what you have.

But the truth is that life works like a savings account in reverse.[6] Zoomed out to the span of an entire life cycle, you see that no one is actually stockpiling anything. You're spending down,

---

6. I owe this image to Kathryn Schulz, "When Things Go Missing: Reflections on Two Seasons of Loss," *The New Yorker* online, February 13 and 20, 2017, http://www.newyorker.com/magazine/2017/02/13/when-things-go-missing.

not saving up. Everything you have—your healthy body, your marketable skills, your sharp mind, your treasured possessions, your loving relationships—will one day be everything you've lost.

If the comprehensiveness of loss is abstract for you, I believe it's useful to practice paying careful attention to the experiences of people who have lived before you. Note the life arc of someone from history or an elderly person you're close to. You must learn to think of the past as populated by people like you, who lived lives like yours, and whose experience was in some ways a forecast of what yours will be.

Before I began my work as a pastor, I trained as a historian. For the most part, historians study lost worlds. They study places, ideas, and ways of life that are different from what exists now. At their best, historians empathize before they explain. You have to believe that the lives others lived were as real and meaningful to them as your life is to you. So you internalize something of the people and places you study. You assume your subjects' perspective on things and imagine how the world appeared to them and why. You feel like you know them. They are more than answers to exam questions. They are people to you. They are people *like* you. Their worlds were just as full of meaning to them as yours is to you. But historians study worlds full of meaning that have disappeared.

Seeing yourself in the losses of others gets easier when what you're observing is not dusty old photographs of nameless faces but the aging process of people you love. A helpful discipline for seeing the truth about loss is to pay careful attention to the elderly people in your life.

My maternal grandmother was a deeply nostalgic woman. She lived a wonderfully full life, and she knew her life was full as she was living it. When I was a child, her home was densely populated with breakable antiques and mementos—a shrine of sorts to her family's history, to their connection with those before them, to all the wonderful times they'd shared. She was always the one following us kids around with a camera, always trying to grab hold of those moments and make them last. Her albums and her shelves and her walls were full of sixty-plus years of family photos.

One photo in particular stands out to me as a picture of her life in all its fullness. It's a photo of my grandparents sitting on the floor of their home in front of a Christmas tree. They look to be about my age. They are both beaming. It's not hard to imagine the world of meaning to which that one captured moment belonged. That Christmas all four of their children still lived at home. I can imagine what fun they must have had picking out gifts for their kids that year. I can imagine the memories they made decorating that tree in the background. I can imagine what sorts of music they played from the turntable on the right side of the frame, and what the house must have smelled like when she was baking all the usual holiday treats.

This picture belongs to a world in which my grandmother could reach out and touch her husband, where she could see his smile, where she could hear the sounds of her children laughing together. It's a picture of her joy in a season of life when she had most everything she'd hoped for from life.

But I never knew that version of my grandmother. By the time I was born, the world of that picture had already begun to crumble. She lost one of her sons a few years before I was born, and I watched her losses continue to mount throughout my childhood. To be closer to my family as they aged, she and my grandfather eventually moved from the community where they'd built their life for decades. That move meant losing the home she loved, their church, their long-term friendships, and all the familiar milestones in their world. I watched her mourn the death of another son and, eventually, her husband. Then, as her own health declined, I watched her lose her independence completely.

About a year before she died, at Christmastime, my grandmother moved into a nursing home. She had left her deeply personal home, full of meaningful objects uniquely hers, for a shared room, a single twin bed, and a small bedside table. Everything in the room issued by management, everything identical to every other room.

When I first visited her there, I couldn't help seeing her with that old Christmas picture as the backdrop, knowing how badly she must have longed to return to that world. What had been a beautiful image of her fullness had become a haunting reminder of everything she had lost. Those things that had been such wonderful sources of joy had become reasons for deep, painful grief. The ravaging effects of time and death had reduced that beautiful world of meaning to ink and paper and fading memories.

When you love someone who is near the end, someone from whom death has stolen so much of life, it is easier to see one who has gone before you as your "forward scout in the wilderness of time."[7] In other words, it's easier to recognize your solidarity with the losses of others and to recognize what losses are awaiting you. It's easier to react to losses of others not with pity but empathy and foresight—to use the experience of the elderly as a lens for viewing what's happening to your life now.

We have to learn to slow down our normal race through our responsibilities and recognize that things are changing. Nothing has made this reality clearer or more heartbreaking for me than watching my children grow up with breathtaking speed. Like my grandmother before me, I'm now taking photos of my own—pulling instants from days full of meaning, freezing them and preserving them while their context fades away. Already I'm

---

7. John Updike, *Problems and Other Stories* (New York: Knopf, 1979), 251.

forgetting more than I remember. Looking back at photos even just a year or two old, I can't remember my kids looking the way they did, much less the way their voices sounded or the quirky things they'd say or the books they wanted me to read on repeat or the sorts of things we'd do to pass the time on all those normal evenings together.

Everyone says these will be the happiest years of my life. I can see why that's true. But these years are slipping away like grains of sand between my fingers. The pictures I'm taking of my kids now, of these beautiful moments I'm enjoying right now, will one day be to me what that Christmas photo became to my grandmother. These photos will be mementos of wonderful times. But they will also be memorials to what I've lost.

Roughly a year ago, during a month's stay in Cambridge, England, I took a picture of my two oldest sons, who were five and three years old at the time, in front of what's known as the Corpus Clock. This clock was one of their favorite things about Cambridge, and it's not hard to understand why. Unveiled in 2008, the Corpus Clock is set in the wall of an old building just across the main street from King's College. The clock includes some of the basic elements you'd expect; it's covered in shiny brass, a pendulum at the bottom swings with the seconds, and its round face with lights marks the minutes and the hours. But there's also a ring around the clock's face that rotates click by click with each passing second. And on top of that ring is perched a hideous mechanical locust. The whole mechanism operates when the arms of this locust reach forward, grab the ring, and pull it in toward its devouring mouth. Every passing second feeds its never-satisfied appetite.

Looking at the beautiful smiling faces of my kids in that photo, seeing how much they've changed even in the year since I took it, it's impossible to miss the metaphor in that grotesque locust just above their heads. For a five-year-old boy, what's not to love? But for those of us who take the point? It's a perfect, haunting image of how time works. Like a swarm of locusts on a newly sprouted field, time is devouring everything I love in this world.

This is what death does. And not just to the elderly or the terminally ill. This is what death does to everyone. Death makes loss normal, universal, and inescapable.

Facing the Problem: How Can We Truly Enjoy Anything?

When you learn to associate time with death, when you pay attention to what time has done to everyone who has gone before you, when you start to recognize what time is doing to your life now, you realize why Ferry framed the study of philosophy the way that he did. Philosophers care about living well in the world as it is. The truth about the world is that everything good that comes into our lives eventually goes out of our lives. "To live well, therefore, to live freely, capable of joy, generosity and love, we must first and foremost conquer . . . our fears of the irreversible."[8]

Fears of the irreversible threaten to destroy our ability to enjoy anything in the present. On the one hand, our hearts are pulled toward the past. Our problem with the past isn't just the bad things we can't undo or make ourselves forget. We struggle just as surely with the pleasant memories. Time makes of them lost worlds we long to recover. We will always be tempted to shrink our lives down to the size of what we've lost, struggling to fully savor the sweetness of what we still have. The joy I have in my son as a six-year-old comes tainted with the loss of my son as a two-year-old. That season of our lives together was precious. Now it's over. It's not coming back. That's the problem of the past.

---

8. Ferry, *Brief History of Thought*, 5.

On the other hand, the future is a problem too. I can't enjoy my son at six years old without knowing that he'll soon be sixteen, or even that the difference between sixteen and sixty is nothing but a breath of air on a cold morning, there for a minute then gone. Once we have learned that time never gives without also taking away, our knowledge of future loss can destroy joy in the present. It unleashes a poison throughout our experience of the good things we have now. How can you truly enjoy anything when you know you will lose it?

Earlier I described our lives not as a savings account that keeps on growing over time but as a reverse savings account from which we keep spending things down. Perhaps a credit card would be an even better metaphor. Everything we enjoy now, we'll have to pay for later. Under the shadow of death, even the wonderful blessings of life make us vulnerable. We don't get to enjoy the beauty of this world without exposing ourselves to the pain that comes when things change. And things always change. Our love attaches us to things that will eventually be torn away.

We often focus on what we don't yet have. We believe the key to our happiness lies in gaining more of what we want. But when we learn to recognize the ubiquity of loss, we come to see that our problem is greater than we imagined. Even if you get everything you want out of life, everything you believe you need to be fully happy, in the end it will never be yours. The more you have, the more you have to lose. And the more you love what you have, the more deeply it hurts when you lose it.

Some people argue that, as one author put it, "the transience of life is the engine of its meaning."[9] In other words, the fact that

9. Andrew Solomon, "'The Good Death,' 'When Breath Becomes Air,' and More," *New York Times* online, February 8, 2016, https://www.nytimes.com/2016/02/14/books/review/the-good-death-when-breath-becomes-air-and-more.html?_r=0/. Schulz makes a similar point in "When Things Go Missing": True, everyone loses everything, "but why should that matter so much? By definition, we do not live in the end: we live along the way. . . . Disappearance reminds us to notice, transience to cherish, fragility

life won't last is the reason to enjoy it as long as it does. There would be no reason to savor every bite of premium ice cream if the bowl were infinitely large. Knowing that the portion size is small and the cost is high motivates us to pay attention, to notice every detail and slowly savor every taste. In this way of thinking about death and loss, recognizing impermanence actually nurtures joy.

I can see that there's something to this way of coping with death, but on the whole I don't buy it. I think the French philosopher Michel de Montaigne was closer to the mark. Fairly early in his career Montaigne published what would become a famous essay called "To Philosophize Is to Learn How to Die." He believed the point of philosophy is to maximize pleasure in life. And of all the hindrances to pleasure in life—whether poverty, suffering, sickness, or whatever else—death is the one that affects every person who ever lives. So the highest goal of philosophy is to figure out how to live with pleasure despite knowing that life ends in death.

Montaigne suggests we imagine a group of condemned criminals being led to the place of their execution. Imagine that along the way the prisoners are led through a number of fine houses, offered any and every enjoyable experience they might wish for: exquisite entertainment, delicious food, anything. "Do you think they can enjoy it or that having the final purpose of their journey ever before their eyes will not spoil their taste for such entertainment?" In other words, what would imminent death do to the criminal's appetite for pleasure? How could he enjoy any of these delicacies when he knows everything is about to end? He couldn't, at least not fully. Instead, "he inquires about the way; he counts the days; the length of his life is the length of those roads. He is tortured by future anguish."[10]

to defend. Loss is a kind of external conscience, urging us to make better use of our finite days."

10. Michel de Montaigne, "To Philosophize Is to Learn How to Die," in *The Complete Essays*, trans. and ed. M. A. Screech (New York: Penguin, 2003), 91–92. Montaigne's bleak

Montaigne's point is that knowing your journey ends in death steals your appetite for anything you might enjoy along the way. If you imagine your life as one long last meal, the selection may be tailored exactly to your tastes, the seasoning may be just right, the texture and temperature may be cooked to perfection, the presentation may be beautiful, but every bite will leave a bitter taste. When you know it's your last meal, you know every bite you take brings you one bite closer to the end.

When you open your eyes to the reality of loss—not the exceptional and tragic and unexpected disruption of life, but the universal and absolute siphoning of time and decay—you come to see that death is a guest at every party. Every good thing comes tainted.

Living with the expectation of loss isn't morbid or dangerous. It's simply realistic. But it can be a crushing burden to carry. Once we've learned to recognize the inevitability of loss, we're forced to confront crucial questions: How can we learn to live well, to enjoy the good things of this world, if we know that everyone loses everything they love? How do we live when we know that the more we love these things, the more it will hurt us to lose them? Is there any alternative to heartbreak on one hand or stoic detachment on the other? How do we conquer our fears of the irreversible, so that knowing we're going to lose everything doesn't keep us from enjoying anything?

Reading the Signs: Jesus Came to Give Life

When we've learned to feel the weight of these questions, we're ready to understand why Jesus, when he described what he came to offer, spoke so often of eternal life. The sweetness of those words—*eternal life*—can be difficult to taste in our time and place. When we're fixated on or overwhelmed by what we're facing here

---

perspective lightened a bit later in life, as subsequent essays in this collection attest.

and now, talk of eternal life can sound otherworldly. Maybe irrelevant at best, escapist at worst. These words seem to describe something far removed from what we think we need. Talk of eternal life can feel like a distraction from real and pressing concerns we have about this life.

Most people who first heard Jesus speak these words didn't respond any more positively than we do. But when we think carefully about death and how it swallows up what we love about life now, we're prepared to see that what Jesus offers is what we've needed all along. Jesus offers eternity, the promise of deathless life, to all who trust in him. And that means he offers joy that won't be clouded by sorrow.

In this section I want to show the centrality of life to the way John's Gospel unfolds its portrait of Jesus. I want to clarify the importance of the problem of loss as context for the purposes of Jesus. But to recognize this connection, and to understand why John frames Jesus's promises the way he does, it's important to begin with a prophecy from Isaiah that lies just beneath the surface of the story John tells.

Isaiah 25 and the Meaning of Eternal Life

Isaiah 25 records a powerful, beautiful promise of a new world full of joy and free from sorrow. The prophecy begins with a feast set by God himself—a worldwide, epic party—and at this feast death itself is swallowed up.

> On this mountain the LORD of hosts will make for all peoples
>> a feast of rich food, a feast of well-aged wine,
>> of rich food full of marrow, of aged wine well refined.
> And he will swallow up on this mountain
>> the covering that is cast over all peoples,
>> the veil that is spread over all nations.
>> He will swallow up death forever;

and the Lord God will wipe away tears from all faces,
> and the reproach of his people he will take away from all
>> the earth,
for the Lord has spoken. (Isa. 25:6–8)

Working our way from the end of this promise to its beginning, notice how closely God's promises in this text fit with the problem of loss we've profiled so far. There's the promise that God will wipe away tears from all faces. In this new world, there will be only comfort and restoration. No heartbreak. No grief. No occasion in which our love exposes us to pain.

Then there's the promise that the Lord will swallow up death forever. Don't miss the irony. Death's appetite is never satisfied. It devours everything from everyone. But on this day death itself will be swallowed up forever. The Lord must do this before he can wipe away every tear from every face. Anything less would be a temporary reprieve. Death is the force behind our tears.

Notice the images the prophet uses to describe death. It is a covering cast over all peoples. It is a veil spread over all nations. These are powerful descriptions of what death does to us. Think of death as a canopy that casts its shadow over all of our lives. It is a blanket that suffocates our joy. It is a barrier, a sort of lid, that cuts us off from the unending, expansive pleasure in life's good things that all of us were meant to crave. This is the veil that God has promised to swallow up, so that God can do away with our sorrow.

But the final promise to notice is the feast. God has promised to do more than remove our sorrow and its cause. He has promised to swallow up death, to cast off the veil, so that he can throw for us a party that will never end. The symbol he's given for the deathless world he has promised is robustly physical. It's not a spiritual realm of disembodied, impersonal floating spirits. It's a world best imagined as a joyful feast. Not Montaigne's last meal, where every bite foreshadows the final bite, but a feast that is joyful precisely because there's no reason to dread the end.

I love the way Jonathan Edwards captures this aspect of heaven's beauty:

> They shall know that they shall forever be continued in the perfect enjoyment of each other's love. They shall know that God and Christ will be forever, and that their true love will be continued and be fully manifested forever, and that all their beloved fellow saints shall live forever in glory with the same love in their hearts. And they shall know that they themselves shall ever live to love God, and love the saints, and enjoy their love. They shall be in no fear of any end of this happiness, nor shall they be in any fear or danger of any abatement of it through weariness of the exercises and expressions of love, or cloyed with the enjoyment of it, or the beloved objects becoming old or decayed, or stale or tasteless. All things shall flourish there in an eternal youth.[11]

Richard Bauckham argues that this passage from Isaiah 25 lies behind the way John unfolds who Jesus is and what he's come to do.[12] In particular, Isaiah's connection between feasting and the triumph of life over death helps us understand the significance of several of John's signs. The first half of John's Gospel is built around a series of "signs" Jesus performed to show what his kingdom would be like. Commentators have offered some helpful images for how these signs work in John. One writer says the signs are like "parables of the nature of his work."[13] N. T. Wright

---

11. Jonathan Edwards, "Heaven Is a World of Love," in *The Sermons of Jonathan Edwards: A Reader*, ed. Wilson Kimnach, Kenneth Minkema, and Douglas Sweeney (New Haven, CT: Yale University Press, 1999), 257–58.

12. Richard Bauckham, *Gospel of Glory: Major Themes in Johannine Theology* (Grand Rapids, MI: Baker Academic, 2015), 182–83.

13. Leon Morris, quoting Edwyn Hoskyns, in *The Gospel According to John*, rev. ed., New International Commentary on the New Testament (Grand Rapids, MI: Eerdmans, 1995), 610n73.

describes the signs as clues on a treasure hunt.[14] They point the way, step by step, to the new world Jesus came to bring in.

Other Gospels have Jesus doing incredible things like exorcisms and calming of storms and healing of all sorts of ailments. They report miracles. But John doesn't report miracles in the usual sense. The signs aren't just impressive displays of power. They are symbols of something deeper. John chose to relate these specific signs not just to show us *why* we can trust Jesus but also so we would know what we're trusting him *for*.[15]

John 2 opens with Jesus and his friends attending a wedding in a town called Cana, not far from where Jesus grew up. The basic details are straightforward. Jesus, his mother, and his disciples have all been invited to this wedding. Perhaps it was a close family friend. In this culture, as in ours, weddings were momentous affairs laced with opportunities for honor or shame. We're immediately brought into the crisis Jesus's friends are facing: this wedding has run out of wine. It's not a trivial problem. This sort of gaffe could expose the groom's family to a lawsuit by the bride's family.[16] The shame involved was devastating. Surely this is what Jesus's mother fears when she comes to her son. Mary's simple statement to Jesus is a plea for help: "They have no wine" (John 2:3). Her simple statement to the nearby servants is a beautiful summary of faith: "Do whatever he tells you" (2:5).

In response to her faith, Jesus acts. Somewhere in the vicinity are six water jars. "Fill the jars with water," Jesus says to the servants, and they do it (v. 7). We aren't told exactly how the trans-

---

14. N. T. Wright, *John for Everyone, Part 1: Chapters 1–10* (Louisville: Westminster John Knox, 2004), 20.

15. In the Synoptic Gospels Jesus's miracles carry symbolic weight too, but the symbolic purpose is more overt in John and closely tied to his selection of which miracles to include. Here's how D. A. Carson explains John's preference of "sign" over "miracle": "Jesus' miracles are never simply naked displays of power, still less neat conjuring tricks to impress the masses, but signs, significant displays of power that point beyond themselves to the deeper realities that could be perceived with the eyes of faith" (*The Gospel According to John*, The Pillar New Testament Commentary [Grand Rapids, MI: Eerdmans, 1991], 175).

16. Carson, *Gospel According to John*, 169.

formation happens. But there is no doubt that it happens by the same authority that spoke the world into being. John has already told us that's who Jesus is (John 1:3). Jesus tells the servants to draw out some of the water and take it to the master of the feast. What they bring the master is a wine so fine the master almost scolds the bridegroom: "Everyone serves the good wine first, and when people have drunk freely, then the poor wine. But you have kept the good wine until now" (2:10).

This might seem like an odd place to begin mounting a case for faith in Jesus. It's a single wedding in an obscure town, and what Jesus does is seen by only a few people. John hasn't chosen this story for its spectacular effects. Jesus would go on to do plenty of things far more impressive than this. Some of those who saw this sign firsthand still didn't believe in him.

Why start here? John chose to begin with this story for the same reason Jesus chose to perform this miracle in the first place. It is chosen because it's like a calling card. It shows what Jesus is all about. Packed into what may seem like a little random or offhanded showboating is a concentrated version of everything Jesus came to do.

Remember that John reports this story as one of his carefully chosen signs—a parable of Jesus's work, a clue in a treasure hunt that leads us on to the new world of life and joy he came to establish. And this is the first of his signs, which makes it a primary window into what his mission is all about. What did he do? He came to a feast that was ending too soon, and by his power he took the party to another level.[17]

By this sign, so relatively unimpressive and seen by so few, Jesus is picturing the deliverance of Isaiah 25—the feast spread out for all peoples. Under the veil of death all of our joys run dry.

---

17. I appreciate and have drawn from the way Tim Keller explains this sign in *Encounters with Jesus: Unexpected Answers to Life's Biggest Questions* (New York: Dutton, 2013), 58–80.

They are real, even beautiful, but they don't last. He has come to cast off that veil once and for all, to blow the lid off the joys of his people. He has come to bring an altogether new taste of his goodness, one untainted by the threat of loss. By this sign, Jesus announces the purpose of his coming: to provide an eternal life of joy.[18]

Following the sign of John 2, "life" becomes central to how the Gospel describes who Jesus was and what he came to do. Already this first sign, alluding to Isaiah's promise, prepares us to see what Jesus means by eternal life. Bauckham notes that in John Jesus barely ever refers to the kingdom of God. It's a major theme in all the other Gospels, but John emphasizes eternal life instead. In John's Gospel, eternal life is a stand-in that describes what sort of world God's kingdom will be.[19] Bauckham defines eternal life in John as "life beyond the reach of death." Throughout this Gospel Jesus, both through what he says and through what he does, insists that he has come to establish a world free from death's grip—a deathless life. "But death," Bauckham continues, "manifests itself not only in the final loss of life, but also in all that damages and impairs life before death. So eternal life is the healing and transfiguration of life in all the ways that mortal life falls short of life in its fullness." Eternal life is "the fulfillment of all that is good."[20] In other words,

---

18. For the connection between John 2 and Isaiah 25, see Bauckham, *Gospel of Glory*, 182–83.

19. Bauckham, *Gospel of Glory*, 192. Bauckham sees Jesus's conversation with Nicodemus as the key link between the kingdom of God, where their conversation begins (John 3:3), and eternal life, where their conversation ends (3:16). D. A. Carson makes a similar connection between the kingdom of God and John's focus on life without prospect of death: *The Gospel According to John*, 188–89.

20. Bauckham, *Gospel of Glory*, 71. See also Moody Smith, *The Theology of the Gospel of John* (Cambridge: Cambridge University Press, 1995). Smith says eternal life is a New Testament theme but especially prominent in John, where it is a present possession but predicated on a future promise of life that death cannot end: "The eschatological goal, the essence of salvation, according to the Fourth Gospel is life . . . , or eternal life. While the eschatological life which God imparts through Jesus Christ occupies an important place in other New Testament books (cf. Matthew 19:29; Romans 6:23), it is particularly prominent in the Gospel of John and 1 John (John 1:4; 3:14–16; 20:30;

the promise of eternal life aims directly at the problem of loss as we've described it. It's more than a reference to quantity of life—a life that goes on and on forever. It's also a reference to quality—a life beyond the reach of anything that holds back our joy in the things God has given.

John 6 and What Blinds Us to Jesus

From the wedding at Cana, John's narrative continues to unfold Jesus's plan to provide deathless, joyful satisfaction to anyone who believes in him.[21] It's a theme that builds to Jesus's final sign, the raising of Lazarus, and perhaps his most powerful statement about who he is—"I am the resurrection and the life" (John 11:25). But along the way there is another sign that, like the one at Cana, ties Jesus's purpose directly to the deathless feasting of Isaiah 25. And in Jesus's words to his followers, helping them understand where his signs are pointing, we get both a warning of what blinds us to his work and a description of what it takes for us to see him clearly. John shows us why clear-eyed honesty about what death

1 John 1:1–2). Exegetes have often observed that according to John eternal life is not only the object of future hope, but already a present possession (5:24; 11:24–25). This is certainly true, but one should also remember that the overcoming of death applies first of all to physical death (5:28-29; 11:1–44) and that the possession or gift of eternal life in the believer's present existence is integrally related to the assurance of its permanence (14:1–4; 17:24)" (149).

21. This theme—eternal life—appears at the conclusion to his conversation with Nicodemus about the kingdom and who will see it. He has come on a mission of God's love so those who believe "should not perish but have eternal life" (John 3:16). It appears again in his conversation with a Samaritan woman in chapter 4—a woman who had been through five husbands, who was now with a sixth man, and who, Jesus knew, had been trying to quench her thirst in wells that would always dry up. "Jesus said to her, 'Everyone who drinks of this water will be thirsty again, but whoever drinks of the water that I will give him will never be thirsty again. The water that I will give him will become in him a spring of water welling up to eternal life'" (4:13–14). And it appears again in chapter 5, where Jesus describes what his Father is doing in the world—raising the dead and giving them life—and how the Son joins him in the work. "Truly, truly, I say to you, whoever hears my word and believes him who sent me has eternal life. He does not come into judgment, but has passed from death to life. Truly, Truly, I say to you, an hour is coming, and is now here, when the dead will hear the voice of the Son of God, and those who hear will live" (5:24–25). Eternal life is the thread that binds his work together.

does to what we love is the path to full-hearted longing for the life Jesus promises.

John 6 tells the story of Jesus feeding five thousand people with nothing more to work with than the light snack of a little boy. It's the only one of Jesus's miracles reported in all four Gospels. But in John's story, the sign sets up a conversation on food that won't run out, that fully satisfies, and that's available only in Christ.

This sign reinforces the same point made at Cana. But this time it's to clear away a misunderstanding just as common among our generation as it was among Jesus's first hearers. Jesus came to offer what we must have if we're to know true and lasting joy. He offers what we can't do without. But what he offers is often far different from what we think we need. We're often focused on what we want from this life. But Jesus doesn't promise to give us more of what death will only steal anyway. He wants to give us what death can't touch.

What happens after Jesus's miracle warns us that it's possible to believe in his power but miss his purpose. It is possible to believe in him, even look to him, on one level, but not on the level that truly matters. The crowds immediately see Jesus as a means to their ends. They're attracted to his power and to the prospect that he might use his power for their purposes. They want to make him king (John 6:15). Surely they want him to free them from Roman occupation. And by the next morning they merely want him to feed them again. All of their desires make sense, and they weren't wrong about his power. They were simply wrong to assume he would use his power to give them what they already wanted.

On the morning after his miracle, when the crowds are hungry again and finally able to track him down, Jesus says to them: "You are seeking me, not because you saw signs, but because you ate your fill of the loaves" (John 6:26). Translation: you've seen my power but missed my point. You ate the bread but missed the sign. In short, Jesus is telling them that their desires are misplaced and constrained by what's here and now and temporary. They only want more of what they will ultimately lose. He wants to give them something altogether different, something that will satisfy them on an entirely different level. "Do not work for the food that perishes, but for the food that endures to eternal life, which the Son of Man will give to you" (6:27). What food endures? What has Jesus come to provide if not physical bread, temporary satisfaction? "I am the bread of life; whoever comes to me shall not hunger, and whoever believes in me shall never thirst.... For this is the will of my Father, that everyone who looks on the Son and believes in him should have eternal life, and I will raise him up on the last day" (6:35, 40).

Consider, too, what he says to them a few verses later, contrasting what he came to offer with what Moses offered in the wilderness: "Your fathers ate the manna in the wilderness, and they died" (John 6:49). Jesus isn't content for his people to die with full bellies. The bread he offers isn't what they are expecting, but it has far more power. "This is the bread that comes down from heaven, so that one may eat of it and not die. I am the living bread that came down from heaven. If anyone eats of this bread, he will live forever. And the bread that I will give for the life of the world is my flesh" (6:50–51).

Jesus wants for them and for us a different quality of life. He wants to set us free from hearts and lives aimed only at good things that can't finally satisfy us. He doesn't want to offer more of what we want, knowing full well he can give us all we want and we'll still end up dead.

These words did not land well on those who heard them. "After this many of his disciples turned back and no longer walked with him" (John 6:66). This talk of eternal life—this redirection of their focus from the things they had always wanted—was not what they wanted from Jesus.

But some of them remained. As in the other Gospels, at the critical moment Peter speaks the truth, and in what he says we get a crystal clear word on what anyone who comes to Jesus must look to him *for*. Jesus only makes sense, only tastes sweet, to those who know that what they really need is not more perishable possessions in this life but a deathless life, where joys don't come into our lives only to pass away. Jesus asks his remaining disciples if they too plan to leave him now. Peter answers, "Lord, to whom shall we go? You have the words of eternal life" (John 6:68).

Peter himself doesn't yet fully understand Jesus. He has much to learn, and so do we. But he at least recognizes what all the signs are pointing to. Jesus came to bring a world of eternal life. That's what he offers, nothing less. He won't make sense to those focused on their own agendas, pursuing always what comes next. But to those who know they're dying, who are tired of good things passing away, his words are the only words that ring true.

Embracing death-awareness is how we strip away a heartbreaking attachment to the things of this world. It's how we're weaned from the materialistic standards we would naturally use to evaluate Jesus. Otherwise, like those to whom Jesus first spoke, we'll continue living as if death isn't a problem, and we'll resent the fact that Jesus doesn't offer us more of what we want from life.

If we want to taste our need for what he does promise, so that what our hearts want aligns with what he offers, we need to carefully consider the effect of death on the of-the-moment blessings our hearts desire. Even if we were to get everything we want out of life, we'd end up losing it all. Death separates us from everyone and everything we love. Jesus came to give us eternal life, and nothing less.

Enjoying the Appetizers: How to Love What You Are Going to Lose

I've argued that we must recognize the many faces of death before we can recognize the signs Jesus left us and love the deathless world to which they point. Until we're honest about the pervasive, painful presence of loss throughout our lives, we won't be drawn in by Jesus and his promise of eternal life. We need to see with the eyes of the heart that we have nothing unless we have Jesus. Everything else is passing away.

Earlier in the chapter, I raised what seems to me a common objection to the Christian focus on eternal life. Sometimes talk of eternal life seems like a distraction from the challenges and opportunities and obligations of this life. At best it sounds abstract and otherworldly. At worst it seems escapist, like some sort of excuse to ignore problems of the present. Or, perhaps, a consolation for those too old or sick to have anything left to live for.

I hope by this point it's clear that this objection is dangerously shortsighted and ironically off the mark. If eternal life sounds otherworldly to you, then *you're* the one not paying close enough attention to this world and its concerns. Jesus focuses on eternal life because he is more attuned to what life is like in this world than those who settle for less. In this world everyone loses everything. Eternal life only seems like a distraction from what you *really* want or need if you pretend you're not dying. That's why the objection is shortsighted.

But the objection is also ironic. Jesus's promise of eternal life is actually the one thing that enables true and resilient joy in our experience of good things that don't last. When talk of eternal life seems like a distraction, it's because we've failed to appreciate the tremendous challenge of loss to any joy we might experience in the present. We've failed to honestly confront the questions raised earlier in this chapter. How can we enjoy what we have when we know we're eventually going to lose it?

When we've learned to feel the weight of this question, we're prepared to see the true and wonderful relevance of Jesus's promise for living now. Jesus's language of eternal life, so far from an otherworldly or ascetic distraction from the goodness of this life, turns out to be exactly what we need to make the most of our time under the sun. Jesus's death and resurrection, and his promise that he will give life to us too if we believe in him, reframe how we experience the transient things of this life. The way to fully taste the sweetness of eternal life is not to pull back from enjoying the good things of this life, but to leverage these good and passing pleasures into longing for the endless feast to come.

Loving this life and all its goodness, knowing with truth and honesty that we're going to lose everything, can actually deepen our love for the life to come. Jesus's promise of triumph over death, a resurrection to eternal life, is an invitation to fully enjoy the beauty of life in this world, no matter how fleeting. In other words, the way to deal with the painful problem of loss is not to pull back from loving the transient things, but to press further in. To love them freely for what they are: precious gifts of a Father who loves you, foretastes of glory divine.

It's true that love for this world will break your heart. We need to see that nothing we enjoy in this life is going to survive. Accepting that truth is more than simple realism; it's what keeps us from trusting our lives to what is here for a moment and then gone.

But that doesn't mean we should protect ourselves from loss and heartache by pulling back from enjoying the pleasures of life in the material world—a sort of preemptive strike, a preventative medicine to ward off a painful disease. When you know that you eventually lose everything you love, and that the more you love something the more it will hurt you to lose it, you could respond with detachment. If every good thing loved will eventually be a good thing lost, maybe it's better not to love at all. Better to protect yourself from the inevitable pain than to give yourself to a moment's pleasure. But that's Stoicism. That's Buddhism.[22] That's not Christianity—it's certainly not what Jesus calls us to in John's Gospel.

Remember, Jesus is the Messiah of Isaiah 25. He chose to picture his deliverance with real physical wine better than anyone ever tasted, with a hearty meal of actual food, and with the resurrection of a tangible, living, and breathing human body. His vision is of an all-satisfying, never-ending physical feast where the joy of those feasting will expand on and on and on. There is nothing otherworldly or ascetic about this vision of eternal life, and no call for withdrawal in the meantime.

Unfortunately, and ironically, the Bible's honesty about the danger of trusting temporary things, and its call to set our hearts on the hope of heaven, has been taken as a rejection of joy in this life, when in fact it's the surest path to joy in this life. Consider these sharp words from Ludwig Feuerbach, the powerful nineteenth-century critic, from an essay published in 1844:

> Unfortunate Christian, what a dualistic, mutilated being you are! Because the visible is temporal, you do not want to let yourself be chained by it, you do not want to rest your heart upon it? By the same reasoning, because a flower withers in autumn, do you refuse to enjoy looking at it in the spring? Because day does not last forever, do you refuse to take pleasure in the light of the sun and prefer instead to close your eyes to the glories of this world and remain in eternal darkness? You fool! Are you yourself not a temporal being? Why do you want to run away from what is in essence like yourself? And what

---

22. See Luc Ferry's clear and helpful comparison of Stoicism, Buddhism, and Christianity in their respective responses to death and loss: *Brief History of Thought*, 17–91.

is left to you when you take away the temporal, the visible? Nothing is left except—Nothing. Only death, fool, is eternal; life is temporal.[23]

Feuerbach's challenge is a powerful one, in part because there's some truth in what he says. Just because something won't last doesn't mean it's not worth enjoying. So far so good. But his perspective is also powerfully misguided. He misjudges both Christianity and the threat of loss to any joy in temporal things.

For Feuerbach, focusing on eternal life is foolishness not just because it's not true, but because it keeps you from enjoying temporary things. He sees hope in a life to come as a barrier to joy in this life. But, far from a barrier, hope in the promise of eternal life enables true joy in the transient things now. It's the only thing that can. Otherwise, we'll be held back by our fear of the irreversible. The knowledge that we'll lose what we love will keep us from enjoying what we love while we have it.

Think back to Montaigne's image. The condemned man, aware that every step brings him closer to his death, has no appetite for all the pleasures that cross his path along the way. Imagine a wonderful feast spread before him in a beautiful house, with servants to wait on him and bring him anything his heart desires. It doesn't matter how delicious or filling that last meal may be. Every bite is bitter because every bite brings him closer to the end.

It's a powerful metaphor for what can happen when we've learned to expect the things we love to pass away. And it's a problem Feuerbach's critique doesn't take seriously enough. We may enjoy the flower in spring, but not without the nagging sense that it's going to wither in autumn and that autumn will come with the blink of an eye. The deeper our love for what we

23. Ludwig Feuerbach, "Comments upon Some Remarkable Statements by Luther," in *The Essence of Faith according to Luther* (New York: Harper and Row, 1967), 122–23.

enjoy, the stronger that nagging sense will be. And what about when we're considering not just daffodils or tulips but the innocence of our children, or the sweetness of having them at home, or the simple daily pleasures of a happy marriage, or the presence of dear friends close at hand, or the wisdom of parents merely a phone call away, or the health of our bodies and the freedom to live pain-free? Then the burden of their transience, the burden of knowledge, can become too great to carry. It can suffocate joy altogether.

But what if we could see the goodness of our temporary pleasures from another perspective? What if we could enjoy what we have *now* in the knowledge of what we'll have *then*? What if the promise of eternal life didn't call us to pull away from the transient joys of this life but to press in to these joys as a foretaste of joys to come?

Dietrich Bonhoeffer once wrote to a friend, "It is only when one loves life and the earth so much that without them everything seems to be over that one may believe in the resurrection and a new world."[24] This perspective fits perfectly with what Jesus has promised, and nothing we've said about death-awareness changes anything. Jesus draws our attention to the grave to break our attachment to foolish hope in false gods, but not to pull us back from joy. He would rather return the good things of life to their proper place in our minds and hearts: they are gifts, not gods. We can fully enjoy them, knowing we'll lose them, precisely because we know we don't have to have them. We can open our hearts to temporary pleasures precisely because we don't give our hearts to temporary pleasures. We

---

24. Dietrich Bonhoeffer, "To Eberhard Bethge, 5 December 1943," in *Letters and Papers from Prison, The Enlarged Edition*, ed. Eberhard Bethge (1971; New York: Touchstone, 1997), 157. I found my way to this quote through Stephen Westerholm, *Understanding Matthew: The Early Christian Worldview of the First Gospel* (Grand Rapids, MI: Baker, 2006), 44.

can only love them for what they are, not preoccupied by what they're not, when we love them not for their own sake but for the true fountain of joy from which they flow. They are wonderful conduits to joy in God, to be loved for God's sake for as long as we have them.

In his *Confessions*, Augustine famously warns that our hearts will be restless until they rest in God. "Wherever the human soul turns itself, other than to you, it is fixed in sorrows." He's consistently wary of impermanent things, of the soul's tendency to "become stuck in them and glued to them with love," for, he reminds us, "these things pass along the path of things that move towards non-existence." Warnings like this are a consistent emphasis for Augustine. But with these warnings come positive statements like this one: "Let these transient things be the ground on which my soul praises you, God creator of all." Or this one: "If physical objects give you pleasure, praise God for them and return love to their Maker."[25]

Augustine is pointing us to a realistic but real affection for the beautiful things of this life. We have nothing to fear, no reason to hold back, when what we enjoy in them and through them is the God who never changes. I especially love the way he captures this balance in a passage from *On Christian Teaching*:

> To enlighten and enable us, the whole temporal dispensation was set up by divine providence for our salvation. We must make use of this, not with a permanent love and enjoyment of it, but with a transient love and enjoyment of our journey, or of our conveyances, so to speak, or any other expedients whatsoever . . . , so that we love the means of transport only because of our destination.[26]

25. Saint Augustine, *Confessions*, trans. Henry Chadwick (New York: Oxford University Press, 1991), 61–63.
26. Saint Augustine, *On Christian Teaching*, trans. R. P. H. Green (New York: Oxford University Press, 1997), 27.

"We love the means of transport only because of our destination." What a powerful way to flip Montaigne's image. For Montaigne's condemned criminal, the destination—certain death—is precisely the reason one can't enjoy anything on the journey. The knowledge of death steals his appetite for pleasure. For the Christian, who is promised eternal life by the one who is the Resurrection and the Life, just the opposite is true. Knowing our destination unlocks a new and purer joy in the passing pleasures we experience along the way. These things that don't last don't have to. They are only meant to whet our appetites.

Jesus pictured his salvation as a joyful feast, unmatched and unending. Everything we enjoy in this life, no matter how temporary, we enjoy as an appetizer for that feast to come. An appetizer isn't meant to satisfy someone who is really hungry. Have you ever attended an evening event, expecting a nice dinner, only to find they're serving finger food? Maybe cheese and crackers, a few assorted fruits, perhaps cookies or butter mints? No matter how fine the cheeses or fresh the fruits, you won't fully appreciate the quality of the food. You'll only notice that it's not enough. But an appetizer can be delightful when you know the fine and filling main course is on its way. In that case, you savor every bite for what it is, not fearful of or disappointed by what it isn't. If it's delicious, you'll be sorry to reach the last bite. But you'll know the appetizer has done its job. It has whetted your appetite for what's still to come.

Jesus's death and resurrection have purchased freedom to enjoy what you have even when you know you're going to lose it. Enjoy your vacation even though it'll be over in a flash. Enjoy parenting your preschoolers even though they'll be grown in the blink of an eye. Enjoy your friendships. Enjoy your marriage. Enjoy your productivity at work. Enjoy whatever health you have left in your body. Of course these things won't last. Yes, it will hurt when they're gone. But they don't have to last to be wonderful. They are delicious, God-given, God-glorifying appetizers for the hearty and satisfying meal that's still to come. They are true and worthy foretastes of the banquet spread for all peoples. And Jesus saves the best wine for last.

5

The Problems of Life and the Promise of Glory

When Jesus talked about why some who hear the gospel don't embrace it, using the parable of the sower and the soils, he described some who have their connection to its message choked out by the "cares of the world" (Matt. 13:22). That phrase rings true, doesn't it? There are things we desperately want to obtain or achieve. There are things we desperately want to avoid. There are things we want to gain and things we're afraid to lose. There are possible problems we're afraid of and genuine problems we already have. Compared with the tangible, everyday concerns that fill our view, the gospel can seem remote, even unreal. The cares of this world can choke out the message, preventing a deep, nourishing, rooted, life-giving embrace of God's promises.

Tim Keller talks about our detachment from God's promises in light of the difference between audio and video.[1] Let's say you're in a showroom at a local electronics store. In front of you

1. Timothy Keller, *Prayer: Experiencing Awe and Intimacy with God* (New York: Dutton, 2014), 204.

a massive TV plays a film shot in beautiful high definition. Meanwhile, over the store's loudspeakers an audio feed features music or advertisements. When you have video and audio coming at you at the same time, which one is more likely to capture and hold your attention? It's video every time. You can tune out audio; it's much harder to tune out video.

Now, every day, every one of us will face the promises of God—of mercies new each morning—and we'll face the cares of this world, what I'll call the problems of life. That's not a question; that's a given. The only question is, Which will be in video and which will be in audio? Will our problems or God's promises have the greater hold on our attention and our affections?

When the promises of God are vivid before our minds and warm in our hearts, the problems of life can't compare with what we have in Christ. It's not that the problems go away, or that we pretend they're not there. It's just that they can't outweigh what we've been promised. But how do we get there? How do we get the promises of God in video?

Believe it or not, death-awareness can be a powerful ally in this struggle. One reason the promises of God are in audio more often than video is that the problem of death isn't in video either. It's in crackling, distant, AM-radio style audio, and we keep the volume mostly down.

Throughout this book I've been making an ironic claim: we need to recognize that our problem is far worse than we've admitted so that we can recognize that Jesus is a far greater Savior than we've known. A clear diagnosis of the problem beneath our problems prepares us for the only worthy cure for what ails us. Honesty about death is the only sure path to living hope—hope that can weather the problems of life under the sun, that doesn't depend on lies for its credibility. We must compare our problems with death so we can compare our problems with glory.

Beyond Comparison

Paul calls for this sort of comparison near the end of 2 Corinthians 4, just before he launches into a beautiful passage on longing for resurrection. Here's what he says in 4:16–18:

> So we do not lose heart. Though our outer self is wasting away, our inner self is being renewed day by day. For this light momentary affliction is preparing for us an eternal weight of glory beyond all comparison, as we look not to the things that are seen but to the things that are unseen. For the things that are seen are transient, but the things that are unseen are eternal.

This passage is full of comparisons. He compares the outer self, which is wasting away, with the inner self that is being constantly renewed (2 Cor. 4:16). He compares what is transient (the things that are seen) with what is eternal (the things that are not seen, 4:18). And at the center of this paragraph full of comparisons, Paul draws our attention to affliction, what I'll call the problems of life, and the promise of glory: "For this light momentary affliction is preparing for us an eternal weight of glory beyond all comparison" (4:17).

Imagine one of those old-fashioned scales. Not the sort of scale you keep in your bathroom or step onto at the doctor's office. The sort of scale that has two plates hung from a bar that's balanced on an arm of some kind. On one plate Paul places our affliction. On the other plate he places the glory God has promised all those who are joined to Christ. Compared with the weight of glory, our affliction is light. Compared with eternity, our problems are momentary. *Really*, we ask? What about job loss or broken relationships or cancer? Compared with glory, light. What about lifelong, painful disability? Compared with eternity, momentary.

Isn't This Uncaring?

Because our experience of our problems doesn't feel light or momentary most of the time, we need to be careful not to misunderstand what Paul means. Otherwise we risk dismissing him before we've seen the beauty in what he's saying. Paul is not saying that the problems we face in this life aren't real. He's not even saying they shouldn't weigh heavy on us, or be hard to push through. Paul does not minimize our suffering. Instead, he maximizes glory.

Consider how we might try to minimize some sort of affliction. We might compare it with what someone else is dealing with. We might compare our exhaustion from parenting difficult children with someone else's daily, chronic disease. We might compare our frustration with an unsatisfying job with what it's like to live in war-torn Syria. We might say, to ourselves or to someone else, *Get over it. That's nothing compared with fill-in-the-blank.* Or we might compare what is with what could be. *Sure, that's tough, but it could be so much worse.*

Paul does not try to explain suffering away like we might. Suffering isn't really his focus. He wants our eyes on glory. He wants our hearts feeling its weight. His point isn't that our problems are light or even momentary. It's that they're light and momentary *compared* with the eternal weight of glory.

Paul can say what he says because his eyes are fixed not on what he can see but on the promises of what he can't yet see. He's locked in on glory the way a groom-to-be locks in on a possible engagement diamond.[2] He's focused on its every angle, searching out every trace of beauty, invested in it with all his resources. Paul

2. Ralph Martin says the word has a "nuance of estimating worth of an object" (*2 Corinthians*, Word Biblical Commentary [Nashville: Thomas Nelson, 1985], 92).

is looking more closely at what he can't see than at what he can see. The problems of his life are still there. They just can't hold his attention.

How did he get there? How do we? How do we see what is invisible more clearly than we see what's so painfully visible? How do we get to the place where God's promises are in video, not simply the faded, crackling audio behind the high-definition video of our problems?

Isn't This Unrealistic?

Before we look to Paul's answer, I want to acknowledge our instinctive dislike for this sort of comparison. Maybe Paul is not being callous and uncaring. Still, doesn't it seem like he's being unrealistic about the seriousness of the problems we face? As if comparing the problems of this life to promises of the life to come is joining some zero-sum game, an either/or where to take one seriously means denying or ignoring the other?

The Bible never asks us to pretend life isn't hard or that the hard things about life don't really matter. When Paul spoke of afflictions, he spoke from experiences most of us will never have.[3] The Bible never asks us to lighten up about the problems of life. It asks us rather to take the problems of life more seriously. Or, more accurately, to recognize that the problem behind the problems is more serious than we thought.

The biblical perspective on life in this world has this balance: the problems we face are real. They do matter. But the problems we focus on most aren't our biggest problems. They're derivative. They're symptoms. They're the dark clouds warning of the storm to come. And we need a vision of the storm to come to put the clouds in perspective.

---

3. For examples within this same letter, 2 Corinthians, see Paul's descriptions of his life in 1:3–11; 4:7–12; 6:3–10; 11:16–29.

Paul isn't being unrealistic when he compares our problems with the eternal weight of glory. He's actually being *more* realistic about our problems. We need to pay close attention to his flow of thought. In 2 Corinthians 4:17 he says the afflictions of life aren't to be compared with the eternal weight of glory God has prepared for us. He feels this truth in his heart because he has fixed his eyes not on what he sees around him but on what he can't yet see. Then in verse 18 he explains why he has focused his eyes where he has: "For the things that are seen are transient, but the things that are unseen are eternal."

Before he points our attention to the unseen eternal things, Paul first points our attention to the truth about all visible things. He knows that everything he can see, good and bad, is passing away. That's why he locks in on the promise of glory he can't see. If you want to pay closer attention to glory, so that you see the promises of eternity more clearly than the problems of now, you need to first pay attention to transience. First be honest about death. Then you'll be captivated by glory.

Paul's argument reminds me of a negative-space portrait, where what *is* there is meant to draw attention and bring focus to what *is not* there. What is visible helps you see what is invisible. Think of the FedEx logo, where the space between E and X creates an arrow pointing forward. Or think of the NBC logo, where the pads of color outline the body of the famous peacock. It's like Paul is saying, you want to see what is not visible? Look at what is visible. Pay attention to where it stops short, runs out, dries up. Trace the limits of what you can see, the transient things always passing away, and there you will start to see the shape of the invisible glory still to come.

Glory is notoriously difficult for us to imagine. We can identify the history of the word easily enough. We know its roots refer to something heavy, substantial. We know it took on shades of celebration, affirmation, and fame.[4] But as it's used here, a catchphrase for what God has prepared for those who trust him, it's so abstract that it can be difficult to long for. Paul is helping us cut through some of the abstraction. He's helping us see glory as the opposite of what hurts us and holds us back in this world.

Glory as *not like that* (cf. Rev. 21:3–4). Not transient but eternal. Not vaporous but weighty. Not fragmented and fleeting, but joy fulfilled and forever. Because whatever glory may be like, it is defined by the presence of God himself, apart from whom there is no good thing. Paul's focus recalls that of the psalmist in Psalm 16. His heart is glad. His whole being rejoices. Why? Because God will not abandon him to Sheol. God will not let him see decay. Instead, he makes known the path of life. He gives him pleasure that lasts forever, found only at God's right hand. He gives him fullness of joy, the weight of glory, in the only place it may be found—in God's presence, where what he loves most is what he can't possibly lose.

Now, to return to Paul's train of thought, think back to the image of an old-fashioned scale. In 2 Corinthians 4:17 Paul put glory on one side and our afflictions on the other. In verse 18 he assumes another sort of comparison that comes first and makes the other more attainable. It's as if he's putting the problems of life on one side, and on the other he's placing the transience of all visible things. Whatever the affliction may be, no matter how painful or ongoing, it can't compare with the fact that everything is passing away. When this problem beneath all problems comes into focus, it puts all other problems in a new perspective.

But enough of telling. The point of this chapter is showing. I want to use several common joy-stealing forces in our lives—

---

4. See, for example, R. B. Gaffin Jr., "Glory," in *New Dictionary of Biblical Theology*, ed. T. Desmond Alexander, Brian Rosner, D. A. Carson, and Graeme Goldsworthy (Downers Grove, IL: Intervarsity, 2000), 507–11.

discontent, envy, and anxiety—to illustrate how recognizing the shadow of death in these experiences can help us shine the light of Christ into them. Each of these problems feeds on misplaced comparison. If we want joy despite the problems of life, we need to think carefully about what we're comparing. We need to learn to compare what we're facing now with death, so that we can compare what we're facing with God's promise of glory.

Discontent: Comparing What Is to What Could Have Been

Sometimes I surprise myself with how surprised I am that things aren't always what I want them to be. Not long ago, I realized I'd been griping a lot to my friends about how much it was costing me to heat my home in the winter months. I'm one of the only people in the history of the world to have central heat and air. It's available to me at the push of a button anytime I get cold. But I don't celebrate the fact that I can walk barefoot in subfreezing temperatures. I'm much more likely to complain about my bill doubling a couple of times a year.

It isn't just a problem with my heat bill. My life is full of good things that aren't perfect. That means it's full of opportunities to prioritize the positive or the negative side of what I'm facing. I have three beautiful, healthy children who are sometimes unruly and always exhausting. I have a job I love that is often more difficult or time-consuming than I want it to be. I'm sure you have examples of your own you could add to my list.

This tendency to notice what's wrong more than what's right is a symptom of a deeper problem. It's a sign that, at least subconsciously, we're surprised that the world doesn't fit the pattern we've designed for it. It may be we've established a baseline expectation of comfort, convenience, or control that has no place in a world where the outer things are passing away.

In the modern West, our baseline expectation for what life should be is set higher than at any other time or place. But this new expectation has come with a high cost we may not notice as clearly as we should.

In *The Paradox of Choice*, Barry Schwartz argues that our "culture of abundance" actually feeds our dissatisfaction with what we have.[5] Every day we're confronted with an overwhelming number of choices about how to structure our lives. But with all these options it's tough not to imagine what could have been better if we'd made another choice—especially when we recognize the limitations of what we did choose for ourselves. We're crippled and preoccupied by all the what-ifs.

Schwartz also highlights another unintended consequence of all this choice, one that's even more to my point. Our vast array of choices feeds a sense that life ought to be fully customizable, seasoned perfectly to my tastes. My expectations about how satisfying my choices should be rise far beyond what's truly possible. There's no chance I'm not going to be let down.

Here's how Schwartz put it in the TED Talk version of his argument:

> Adding options to people's lives can't help but increase the expectations people have about how good those options will be. And what that's going to produce is less satisfaction with results, even when they're good results. . . . The reason that everything was better back when everything was worse is that when everything was worse, it was actually possible for people to have experiences that were a pleasant surprise. Nowadays, the world we live in—we affluent, industrialized citizens, with perfection the expectation— the best you can ever hope for is that stuff is as good as

---

5. Barry Schwartz, *The Paradox of Choice: Why More Is Less* (New York: Harper-Collins, 2004).

you expect it to be. You will never be pleasantly surprised because your expectations, my expectations, have gone through the roof.[6]

I don't doubt that contentment has always been a struggle no matter when you've lived or where. But in the modern West we do face some unique and easily ignored obstacles to joy in the good things our lives afford us. Schwartz argues that as our quality of life has improved in so many ways, our baseline expectation has settled somewhere in the neighborhood of perfection. Best-case scenario, we get what we believe is normal, even owed to us. More likely, we feel disappointed.

Schwartz's antidote to this modern disease is interesting. "The secret to happiness," he concludes, "is low expectations."[7] It makes sense, doesn't it? Lower your standard for how enjoyable or satisfying life should be, and you'll be more satisfied with what life is. I believe there is a lot of wisdom in what Schwartz is saying, both about what feeds our discontent and also what it will take to move forward. We need a new baseline expectation for life in the world as it is.

But how do we find our way to more realistic expectations? Here is where I would add one further argument: the path to realistic expectations about life moves through honesty about death. Our detachment from death has carved out the space for our expectations to run wild. The forgotten truth is that even if I could structure every part of my life today exactly the way I want, I can't stop death from stealing everything I have. I may face a range of choices about life that previous generations couldn't imagine. But I cannot choose to be immortal. This limitation casts a shadow over every area of my life.

---

6. Barry Schwartz, "Paradox," March 2017, TEDGlobal 2005, http://www.ted.com/talks/barry_schwartz_on_the_paradox_of_choice/transcript?language=en#t-1149333.

7. Schwartz, "Paradox."

Our perpetual discontent is a sign that, as Augustine put it, we "seek the happy life in the region of death."[8] I don't stop experiencing the effects of mortality just because I refuse to acknowledge its grip. It's just that I'll be surprised by those effects again and again. I'll continue to believe life is as fully customizable as our consumer society has promised me. I'll continue to be surprised when it's not. And at some point I won't just be surprised by the uncontrollable brokenness of the world; I'll be devastated. If I complain about the cost of my heating bill in winter, what will I do with job loss, or type 1 diabetes, or the cancer diagnosis of a child?

So long as our expectations for a tailor-made world go unchecked, we will eventually be blindsided by suffering. And when we are blindsided, we will be tempted to reject the goodness of God that is the only source of true comfort.

Here's what I mean: if my baseline expectation of the world is comfort, convenience, and control—if this is what I assume I'm owed from life—then when I suffer, I will likely blame God. In my frustration or disappointment or pain I may see a sign of his displeasure. Or maybe a sign of his neglect. But one way or another I'll see my suffering as abnormal, and therefore a sign of God's absence from my life. I won't recognize that, in fact, the brokenness I'm experiencing is not a sign of his absence but a primary reason for his presence in Christ.

We sometimes judge the plausibility of God's promises to us in light of what we're experiencing now. We are tempted to believe that if God is allowing us to suffer as we are, we can't trust him to deliver on his promise of redemption, resurrection, and an eternal life of joy with him. We can view his promises as an upgrade to an already-comfortable life, icing on the cake of the

---

8. Saint Augustine, *Confessions*, trans. Henry Chadwick (New York: Oxford University Press, 1991), 64.

pleasant ease that is our baseline expectation. But this is not how his promises come to us in Scripture, and viewed like this his promises will never make sense. If his promises are no more to us than icing on the cake of good lives now, then those promises will always seem irrelevant and otherworldly when we suffer.

But when we recognize death's hold on us and everything we love, we won't be surprised that life isn't what we want it to be. Frustration, disappointment, dissatisfaction—these belong among the many faces of death, the pockets of darkness that make up death's shadow. These experiences are normal, not surprising. Death-awareness resets my baseline expectation about life in the world.

This honesty about death then prepares me for what *is* truly surprising: that God the Son subjected himself to the limitations, brokenness, and death that are normal for us. That he would join me in my experience of the normal trials of life in the valley of the shadow of death. That he would do this precisely so that he can revolutionize what is normal.

The brokenness I experience—the frustration, disappointment, dissatisfaction, pain—is not a sign of God's absence. It is the reason for his presence in Christ. This is why the Word became flesh and dwelt among us (John 1:14). He came because he knows we're thirsty for more than what we've tasted so far (John 4:13–14). He knows that every meal has left us hungry. He came to provide living water, bread of life, full and free satisfaction for all who eat and drink from him (John 6:26–35).

When our eyes are fixed on the weight of this glory, we can experience dissatisfaction or disappointment without discontent. We can embrace what God has given us without preoccupation by what he hasn't given. There's nothing we can't enjoy fully no matter how limited. And there's nothing we can't do without, no matter how sweet.

Envy: Comparing My Experience with Others'

Like discontent, envy is not a uniquely modern problem. But like discontent, it's an age-old problem with a uniquely modern twist.

On one hand, envy or covetousness has a central place in the Bible's unfolding story of human sin and sadness. Think of the first sin, when Adam and Eve chose to eat from the forbidden tree. That decision flowed from envy of God, a belief that he was holding them back and a desire to become more like him (Gen. 3:4–6). Envy motivated the first murder, too, when Cain resented the affirmation and acceptance Abel received for his offering (Gen. 4:3–8). The Ten Commandments round off with a command not to covet your neighbor's wife or his servants or his animals (Ex. 20:17). And the problem of envy surfaces again and again throughout the history of Israel, as they wanted more of what other nations around them seemed to have. They envied other nations' kings. They envied their power and wealth. Ultimately they envied their gods. Envy is no modern problem. It's a basic part of our fallen human condition.

Still, there are forces in our lives today that pour fuel on this perpetual fire. Take, for example, the way we use social media. Donna Freitas, a researcher with Notre Dame's Center for the Study of Religion and Society, spent years studying the effect of social media on the lives of American college students. She talked with students from different regions, different ethnic and socioeconomic backgrounds, and different sorts of campuses. Across all these boundaries one common theme came through: "the importance of *appearing* happy."[9] Students described their social media accounts as highlight reels. Everyone posts only the best things about their lives: the best experiences, the best outfits, the

---

9. Donna Freitas, *The Happiness Effect: How Social Media Is Driving a Generation to Appear Perfect at Any Cost* (New York: Oxford University Press, 2017), 13. Italics original.

best hair days. They even stage looks and experiences precisely so they can post them. Everyone knows this is what everyone else is doing. But knowing it's all for show doesn't stop anyone from joining in the comparison game.

Freitas describes what she found as the "happiness effect": "Simply put, because young people feel so pressured to post happy things on social media, most of what everyone sees on social media from their peers are happy things; as a result, they often feel inferior because they aren't actually happy all the time." Students are comparing the best things about the lives of others to the worst things about their own. Apps like Facebook have become like "the CNN of envy"—24/7 coverage of the wonderful things other people get to enjoy.[10]

This exhausting comparison game isn't just a problem for college students. All of us have a bigger window into the lives of others than any other generation, but it's a limited, heavily filtered window that magnifies our struggle with envy. Envy is a terrible problem not just for what it motivates us to do, but also for how it makes us feel. Few things have more power to steal our joy in what we have than comparing what we have with what others have. Maybe you compare your kids or your spouse with someone else's. Why can't my kids be that well-behaved or that successful? Why can't my spouse have his temperament, or look like her, or make that much time for the kids? Maybe you envy that a friend has a spouse and kids in the first place. It could be that you wish your body looked like someone else's, or that you envy someone's popularity. Sometimes we compare our performance with someone else's abilities or accomplishments. And in our materialistic culture, all of us are prone to comparing our possessions with those of other people. If only I had their house, or their ability to spend money without worry.

---

10. Freitas, *Happiness Effect*, 14, 39.

Paul wrote that covetousness, at root, is always a form of idolatry (Col. 3:5). Just as Israel wanted what others nations had, and turned to the gods of those nations, so we in our envy want what some other god might offer. I think what Paul means is that anytime we envy what others have, we implicitly say that God got it wrong. He should have given me more. Our envy communicates ingratitude for what he has given us. It communicates unbelief in his wise and loving providence. In short, it's us responding to life as if the God of the Bible doesn't exist and therefore isn't trustworthy. We want some other god.

This is where death-awareness becomes useful to us in our fight against envy and for joy in what God has given us. Confronting our envy with the shadow of death is a first step toward confronting our envy with the promises of God.

Let's play out our implicit denial of God a little further. Let's imagine the world as the godless place our envy assumes— a place where we get what we can while we can, by ourselves and for ourselves. In other words, let's imagine this world from the "under the sun" perspective of Ecclesiastes. Remember what the Preacher said about life under the sun? This was a man who had no one to envy because he had everything anyone could want. He had more pleasure, more wealth, and more success than anyone else, so that, as he puts it, "I became great and surpassed all who were before me in Jerusalem" (Eccles. 2:9). In our envy, we're saying we'd be happy if we had what the Preacher had. But he tells us to think again. He had it all, but in the end, all he had was the wind. "There was nothing to be gained under the sun" (2:11).

Why? His reasons are clear and consistent throughout the book. Everything is vanity because everyone dies. If it all ends in death, what's the use? There's nothing gained.

Perhaps you don't share the Preacher's despair. You might argue that, even if we die in the end, I'd still rather make the most of my life while it lasts. Sure, I'm going to die, but I'd rather go to my grave with a nice house, a happy family, or whatever else along the way.

If that's your reaction, join me for this little thought experiment. Imagine two groups taking a transatlantic flight from the United States to the United Kingdom. One group gets stuck on a military-issue cargo jet—one of those flying warehouses without climate control or sound insulation, much less beverage service. This group is stuck sitting on unpadded, flip-up canvas seats without so much as a window to enjoy. The other group takes a luxury private jet. The seats are covered in the softest of premium leathers. The legroom allows for full extension. There's an on-board chef for made-to-order fine dining and a menu of excellent beverages. So far it seems there's a world of difference between these two flights. Who on the cargo jet wouldn't envy the journey of the others?

Now imagine both jets suffer catastrophic engine failure and both jets crash into the Atlantic, killing everyone on board. As each plane nosedives toward certain death, do you believe if you were on the cargo jet you'd care about trading places then? If you knew you'd end up in a watery grave, do you think you'd care whether you died strapped to canvas or calfskin? Whether you died gripping a shoulder harness or fine crystal?

The problem under the surface of our envy is blindness to our true condition. The problem isn't that we don't have what our neighbor has. The problem is that we're hurtling toward death, where everything we have and everything we wish we had will all be wiped away. All our time and energy spent wishing, churning, working over what we don't have that others do—it's all wasted. It's foolishness. It's laughable. Or, in the words of the Preacher, it's nothing but vanity and striving after wind.

This death-awareness can be a powerful weapon for pushing back against envy and its assault on joy. But it's only a first step.

Death-awareness can help unmask the foolishness of our envy, but it can't uproot it. The only lasting solution is a new affection for what God has given and what he has promised give. The only remedy is a heart with stronger love for what is ours through Jesus than for whatever else we may or may not get in this life. Seeing what death says about our envy is most useful as a palate-cleanser that prepares us for the sweet taste of the gospel and the liberating perspective it offers us.

Now, to connect these promises to our struggle with envy, let's adjust our transatlantic flight analogy. Imagine now that you're an American who has won an all-expenses-paid trip to Paris for a month of luxurious vacationing. There are no strings attached. You just need to claim the offer in faith by boarding the plane at the proper time.

Now imagine one scenario in which you get unexpectedly upgraded to a first-class flight. You get a great meal and nicer headphones. You get the temporary sense of superiority over those on the far side of the curtain. You get a good night's sleep in one of those fully reclining seats. And when you wake up, you're in Paris. Who wouldn't appreciate all these upgrades? Who wouldn't see it as yet more evidence of the goodness of the one who promised the trip and made it possible?

Now imagine another scenario. You board the plane in faith, and right away the trouble begins. Because of a storm you can't take off for hours. It's cramped and hot and you're stuck in one of those center-row middle seats between a crying, defecating two-year-old and a large man from a culture that, for all its richness and beauty, doesn't value personal hygiene. After takeoff things only get worse. The bad weather requires a detour. You have to make an extra connection at Dulles before crossing the Atlantic, where you're diverted again through Frankfurt. The meal is inedible. Your puny video screen doesn't work. You get no sleep at all.

It's a rough few hours, no question. No one could blame you for wanting a better experience.

But if you're thinking clearly, you're not caught up in the pain of the moment. You're not a slave to your immediate circumstances. You remember that this temporary suffering doesn't matter as much as the fact that in the morning you'll be in Paris. For a month, for free, you'll enjoy the best that human culture has to offer. You'll spend hours in the Louvre. You'll drink coffee on patios overlooking the Champs Élysées. You'll stroll through the gardens of Versailles and maybe take a day trip or two through the wine country. You sip on this future by faith. And you remind yourself that the thing promised is so great that the temporary suffering along the way doesn't compare.

Now, isn't it true that you'd want this journey whether you got the upgraded travel or not? In fact, you could say that if your journey is the more difficult one, you're able to savor the hope of the destination even more. From the perspective of Paris, the journey and what you did or didn't have along the way isn't less real, or even less painful. But neither is it your most important, most definitive experience. It is put in its place by the glory of your destination.

Death-awareness doesn't remove the differences between our lives and the lives of others. It doesn't mean the things others enjoy that we don't aren't good and worthwhile, even gifts of God to them that we would fully enjoy were they given to us. It simply puts these temporary goods in their place. And it clears a path for the promises of Jesus to take their rightful place in our hearts.

Anxiety: Comparing What You Want with What Might Be

In *The Cost of Discipleship* Dietrich Bonhoeffer offers a crucial insight into the root of our anxiety: "Worry is always directed toward tomorrow."[11] When we're anxious about something, we bring the future and its uncertainties into our experience of the present. "It is our securing things for tomorrow which makes us so insecure today."[12]

Bonhoeffer is commenting on Jesus's teaching on anxiety in Matthew 6. For example: "Therefore I tell you, do not be anxious about your life, what you will eat or what you will drink, nor about your body, what you will put on. . . . Do not be anxious about tomorrow, for tomorrow will be anxious for itself. Sufficient for the day is its own trouble" (Matt. 6:25, 34). Jesus is correcting, and Bonhoeffer is highlighting, our tendency to live out our futures before they arrive. We tend to set our hearts on a future we've imagined for ourselves—a future in which we gain the things we hope for and hold on to the things we have. Our anxiety comes from knowing that the tailor-made future we want for ourselves is beyond our ability to provide and beyond our ability to protect. Though we know intuitively that we can't deliver it, still we try our best. We scheme. We plan. We stockpile. We pursue hard and hold on tight. Bonhoeffer says that our "abuse of earthly goods consists of using them as a security for the next day."[13] But in this focus on tomorrow it isn't just our earthly goods that get abused. We abuse ourselves too, preempting the joy we might have in the goodness of the present.

"Worry is always directed toward tomorrow." That's a clarifying summary, isn't it? Any time I'm afraid or anxious, my heart and mind are directed toward tomorrow, bringing its concerns into today, where they don't belong. But it's one thing to recognize that this is what I'm doing and another thing to resist the urge. How can I live with joy in the present without fear of the future and its uncertainties?

---

11. Dietrich Bonhoeffer, *Discipleship*, Dietrich Bonhoeffer Works, vol. 4 (Minneapolis: Fortress, 2001), 165.

12. Bonhoeffer, *Discipleship*, 165.

13. Bonhoeffer, *Discipleship*, 165.

I believe the key is recognizing that the future is not nearly so uncertain, not so ambiguous, as our fears imply. Our anxieties are fueled by "what-ifs." We must combat the what-ifs with the rock-solid certainty of what-will-be. Two certainties, feeding one off of the other, are especially helpful for sweeping the legs out from under our fears. We will certainly lose everything to death. But in Christ we have a certain inheritance that nothing can threaten. The first certainty exposes our fears as useless and even foolish. The second promises that our fears are absolutely unnecessary. And connecting with the certainty of death is a critical step toward connecting with the certainty of hope.

I've said that our fears come from living in the future before it's arrived. But there is a sense in which our fears come from not looking *far enough* into the future. We typically fear what we may not get or what we may lose tomorrow. We feel as if there's ambiguity involved, as if even if we gained everything we desire, those things might be ours to keep. But in reality if we get what we want, death will take it from us anyway. Death shows us that there is no ambiguity. Loss is not a possibility but a guarantee. And for this reason our fears are all wasted.

I believe this is what Jesus has in mind in Matthew 6:27: "And which of you by being anxious can add a single hour to his span of life?" For all our worrying, we can't change the fact that our lives will end. We're immobilized by the thought of risk, as if there's something ultimately at stake, but death reminds us that we might as well accept that what we fear is guaranteed.

Jesus's question reminds me of a scene in HBO's critically acclaimed World War II series *Band of Brothers*. At one point soon after the Normandy invasion, Lieutenant Ronald Speirs, a notoriously fearless officer, comes across a private, Albert Blithe, who has been completely frozen by fear. The private admits that, as others were fighting around him on D-Day, he had spent the battle hiding alone in a ditch. And this is how Speirs encourages him: "You hid in that ditch because you think there's still hope. But Blithe, the only hope you have is to accept the fact that you're already dead, and the sooner you accept that, the sooner you'll be able to function as a soldier's supposed to function."[14]

It's a powerful point, isn't it? You're immobilized by fear because you haven't accepted that what you're worried about is certainly going to happen. You haven't accepted that you're going to die. You're assuming there's something at stake when, in an ultimate sense, there isn't. So why are you worried?

I'm not denying this is a bleak thought. It's ugly and awful and we ought to hate what it means for our lives. But it's also freeing. It may not be encouraging, but it is at least clarifying: our fears for the future are useless, even foolish, because the future always brings death.

So what then? Should we just give up caring about anything? Of course not. Death-awareness is only the first step in fighting fear with the certainties of what's to come. Death puts our misplaced insecurities in perspective. It warns us against living as if the future were ambiguous, as if we might be able to love transient things and not lose them. And in that sense it prepares us to care more deeply about another certain hope, beyond the transience of this life. Death-awareness purges our affections so we care most deeply about what can't be lost or destroyed.

A little earlier in Matthew 6 Jesus warns against piling up treasure that moth and rust can destroy or that thieves could break in and steal. In time, decay destroys everything, and death is the greatest thief of all. So, Jesus argues, you must place your treasure in heaven, "where neither moth nor rust destroys and where thieves do not break in and steal" (6:20). Do you see what Jesus is doing here? He's using the prospect of decay and loss—

---

14. *Band of Brothers*, "Carentan" (2001).

what will be lost to death—to drive us to love what can never be lost. Accepting the reality of death—bringing it into our daily experience, and especially our fears—is the way to bring the promises of heaven into our daily experience, and especially our fears.

Remembering death helps us stop trying to protect what we can't protect. And remembering Christ helps us stop trying to protect what we don't need to protect. Freedom from fear comes only when we see that what matters most in our future isn't ambiguous at all. There is no reason to remain enslaved.

I believe this liberating perspective is what the author of Hebrews had in mind when he wrote of Jesus's defeat of the one who held the power of death. Hebrews 2:14–18 describes the purpose of Jesus's incarnation as a conquest of death. He had to take on flesh and blood so he could be killable. He had to be killable so that, by his death, "he might destroy the one who has the power of death, that is, the devil, and deliver all those who through fear of death were subject to lifelong slavery" (2:14–15).

Hebrews 2 describes slavery to fear as a basic part of the human condition. And that description fits our experience remarkably well. We may not always recognize death as the specter, but it's always there, threatening us with loss, making us hedge our bets and look for protection, stealing our joy and freedom in life. But in Christ we have no reason to hide. We no longer have to waste our time protecting what can't be protected. We no longer need to hold back what isn't ours to preserve anyway. We're set free.

When our eyes are fixed on the weight of glory, not all the things passing away, we are free to throw caution to the wind and make decisions that seem ridiculous to the world—decisions like that of John Paton, a nineteenth-century Scottish missionary to the New Hebrides islands. The native tribes living on these islands practiced ritual cannibalism. The first missionaries who arrived on these islands were killed and eaten shortly after they reached land. It was less than twenty years later that Paton prepared to sail to the islands with his young wife.

In his autobiography, Paton describes a conversation with a Mr. Dickson, who surely meant well when he tried to convince the young missionary not to take the risk. Dickson pleaded with Paton: "The cannibals! You will be eaten by cannibals!" Translation: *It's not worth it. You've got your whole life in front of you. Think of what you could lose!*

Now see how Paton responded:

> Mr. Dickson, you are advanced in years now, and your own prospect is soon to be laid in the grave, there to be eaten by worms; I confess to you, that if I can but live and die serving and honoring the Lord Jesus, *it will make no difference to me whether I am eaten by Cannibals or by worms*; and in the Great Day my Resurrection body will rise as fair as yours in the likeness of our risen Redeemer.[15]

Paton understood the implications of death. He knew his future was not ambiguous. There was nothing about his life he could protect to begin with. And Paton's eyes were set on glory. The Great Day of resurrection was everything to him. And he knew nothing on this earth could touch that treasure.

Glory: Comparing Now with What Will Be

In his chapter on hope in *Mere Christianity*, C. S. Lewis says that, to make the most of the transient things of earth, "we must learn to want something else even more." It's an ironic claim, but true.

---

15. John Paton, *John G. Paton, Missionary to the New Hebrides: An Autobiography Edited by His Brother* (1889; Edinburgh: Banner of Truth, 1965), 56. I found my way to this quote through the helpful biographical sketch by John Piper: "'You Will Be Eaten by Cannibals!': Courage in the Face of Fierce Opposition," in *Filling Up the Afflictions of Christ: The Cost of Bringing the Gospel to the Nations in the Lives of William Tyndale, John Paton, and Adoniram Judson* (Wheaton IL: Crossway, 2009), 85–108.

"Aim at Heaven and you will get earth 'thrown in': aim at earth and you will get neither."[16] Before we can truly enjoy life in this world—before we can face up to the problems of life in this world in a way that's effective and helpful—we must learn to love glory more than we love this world. We must learn to love glory more than what we might have had in this life. More than what others have. More than what still may or may not come to pass. If we don't want glory more, we will struggle with discontent, with envy, with anxiety, and a host of other cares too many to name.

How do we get to where we want glory more? Through unflinching honesty about what is passing away. Through admitting, with Paul, that the "things that are seen are transient" (2 Cor. 4:18). Death will destroy anything else I set my heart upon. When I accept this harsh reality, of course I'll want glory more.

Paul's call to fix our eyes on what is eternal, to feel the weight of glory God has prepared for those who are in Christ, is not a call to stick your head in the sand. It is not escapist, naive, or unrealistic. It is a call rooted in the morbid truth about life in the world. And it is a call with the power to set us free—free to enjoy and to invest and to celebrate the goodness of what God has given, while we wait for him to make all things new.

---

16. C. S. Lewis, *Mere Christianity* (1952; New York: HarperCollins, 2001), 134–35.

6

Grieve in Hope

Throughout this book, I have tried to establish an ironic claim: facing up to the truth about death can lead us to deeper hope in life. My first goal, then, has been to encourage greater honesty about the facts. Perhaps more than any other culture anywhere in time or space, we in the modern West have detached ourselves from the reality of death. We've lost our feeling for death's sting.

Remember Pascal's image from back in chapter 1? The human condition as a lineup of condemned prisoners, facing execution one by one, every man seeing his own death pictured in the death of every other. We draw back from this image by instinct. It seems unrealistically dark and even dangerous to us now. And even by the standards of his own day, surely, he meant for this image to be jarring. But Pascal took death personally—not as someone else's problem—and in this personal engagement his perspective is far more consistent with the sweep of human history than ours. Far closer, too, to the perspective of the Bible. I've argued that we would be wise to take death personally ourselves—to restore some of our feeling for death's sting.

But honesty is no end in itself. Honesty about death is merely the first step. Honesty should lead us on to grief, and grief should lead us on to hope.

Through Honesty to Grief

There are other ways to face up to death besides grief, of course. There is a dangerous, nihilistic sort of death-awareness that treats grief as nothing but mushy sentimentality. You're going to die. So is everyone you love. Nothing you do will matter and there's nothing you can do to change that. So get over it. There's also a friendlier version of this outlook. Think of the circle of life song in *The Lion King*. No need to deny death. It's perfectly natural, necessary, and life-giving. This sort of death-awareness calls for familiarity and even a kind of friendship with death.[1]

Both of these versions of death-awareness amount to death-acceptance. Sure, they may work against our detachment from death's certainty. They encourage us to face up to the fact that everyone dies and there's nothing we can do about it. But they are fully detached from death's meaning.

I've argued that we must give up pretending, perhaps even believing, that we're not going to die. But that doesn't mean we should make peace with the facts. Yes, you are going to die. So will everyone you love. And yes, that is and should be devastating, heart-breaking news. Death-acceptance is just as dishonest as death-avoidance.

Jesus's posture at the tomb of Lazarus is a powerful model for us here. When he comes to the tomb, he walks into a situation he has orchestrated. He knew Lazarus would die. In a sense he made

---

1. For example, in *Death's Summer Coat*, Brandy Schillace argues that "once we meet death and keep it near, it ceases to threaten us, ceases to be alien. Death, when embraced, can be the means to healing and to progressing through grief for the living. It can also be our greatest means of connection" (*Death's Summer Coat: What the History of Death and Dying Teaches Us about Life and Living* [New York: Pegasus, 2015], 11–12).

sure of it, for his own purposes (John 11:1–6). But when he sees his friends in their grief, his heart is broken. "When Jesus saw [Mary] weeping, and the Jews who had come with her also weeping, he was deeply moved in his spirit and greatly troubled" (11:33). Then, when he reaches the tomb, when he sees with his own eyes the place holding his friend's lifeless body, "Jesus wept" (11:35).

Don't miss the power of this simple statement. Jesus knew Lazarus was going to die. By choosing to delay his visit after news of Lazarus's illness, Jesus even made sure he would die. And Jesus knew exactly what he was about to do. He knew he would speak a word and bring this body back to life. He's in complete control of this situation from beginning to end. But he's not callous. He's not detached from the pain of those he loves. He doesn't scold anyone for weeping. He joins them. The reality of death and its effects on those he loves broke his heart.

Grief over death and all its many faces is the only honest, truthful response to a world that was not made to be this way. Grief tells the truth about the goodness of what God has given us. It's how we agree with Jesus about the offensiveness of death's challenge to everything that is good and right and beautiful. Grief is not unbelief in what God will do. It isn't ingratitude for what God has done. Grief is simply honest, even Christlike.

If you choose to embrace death-awareness, you should know this is also a choice to welcome grief into your life. And not just when you're standing next to the hospital bed or near the graveside. I mean grief as a daily companion. Anything less ignores the gap between what God has promised and what we experience now.

Through Grief to Hope

So, death-awareness, for the Christian, should lead to grief, not to some sort of callous death-acceptance. But grief itself is a means to an end. We mourn because that's a truthful response to the brokenness of the world as we experience it. But we don't grieve as those who have no hope (1 Thess. 4:13). If you'll pardon a mixed metaphor, we need to feel death's sting so that we can taste the sweetness of resurrection.

Augustine describes a surprising similarity between sorrow and dung. In the wrong place at the wrong time for the wrong purpose, both sorrow and dung defile whatever they touch. But in the right context, both can become fruitful, life-giving fertilizer. Grief can become the soil where living hope takes root and grows strong.[2]

Think of grief as a kind of telescope. To the naked eye perhaps the promises of Jesus seem small, beyond my frame of view, remote and disconnected from what I see around me. They belong to some other world than the one I'm living in. But when I learn to see the painful truth about death, that begins to change. When I use my grief as a telescope, looking through it to grab hold of his image, Jesus comes forward and into focus, blown up to size so that he dominates my entire frame. The promise of life makes the pain of grief not a terminal condition but a transitional one. Grief is not a dead end but the necessary pathway to Jesus, a valuable means to a blessed end, a tool to be repurposed and fully leveraged.

Grief Clarifies What We Are Hoping For

There is a kind of grief that leads to despair. In a *New Yorker* essay titled "When Things Go Missing," Kathryn Schulz draws a fascinating comparison between what it feels like to lose some objects—your keys, your phone, your wallet—and what it feels like to lose what you love through death. "With objects, loss im-

---

2. Augustine's sermon is cited in George Guthrie, *2 Corinthians*, Baker Exegetical Commentary on the New Testament (Grand Rapids, MI: Baker, 2015), 377.

plies the possibility of recovery; in theory, at least, nearly every missing possession can be restored to its owner." You just have to figure out where you left your phone, or who might have picked up your wallet. "That's why the defining emotion of losing things isn't frustration or panic or sadness but, paradoxically, hope." We feel that what's lost is merely on the way to being found. But when it comes to relationships lost to time, or precious people lost to death, "loss is not a transitional state but a terminal one. Outside of an afterlife, for those who believe in one, it leaves us with nothing to hope for and nothing to do. Death is loss without the possibility of being found."[3]

Schulz is exactly right about what death means without the hope of an afterlife. There is no recovery. No redemption. No possibility of finding what you've lost. It's a terminal condition, not a transitional one. Finding, having, loving, enjoying—those experiences are unusual, transitional. Only loss is normal, terminal. And this means that grief over what has been lost is always tethered to the past. It is a prison that traps us, keeps us chained to what was, and bars us from joy in what is. Or, to shift metaphors, grief is like a paddle we use to fight back against time's ever-rolling stream.

But if Jesus can offer eternal life to those who are losing everything, then oh how different our grief becomes. It doesn't go away, because it shouldn't. But it is channeled into hope. In Christ our grief gains an aim, a new direction: grief gives rise to hope.

One of my favorite things about C. S. Lewis's essay "The Weight of Glory" is the way Lewis reorients how we think about nostalgia. We normally think of nostalgia as a sort of prison where our hearts are chained up by a longing to go back, always

3. Kathryn Schulz, "When Things Go Missing: Reflections on Two Seasons of Loss," *The New Yorker* online, February 13 and 20, 2017, http://www.newyorker.com/magazine/2017/02/13/when-things-go-missing.

back. But Lewis argues that nostalgia is not really a longing for what we had, but a longing for more. Nostalgia, for the Christian, carries our hearts toward the world to come.[4]

This is how death-awareness carries us to clearer and deeper hope in what God has promised us. To long for the world to come, we need hearts and minds that recognize the truth about this world and cry out, *No more!* That's why, when Revelation 21 describes the beauty of the new Jerusalem, it does so in negative terms. It's a place where every tear is wiped away, a place where "death shall be no more, neither shall there be mourning, nor crying, nor pain anymore" (Rev. 21:4).

So long as we are numb to death's sting, the notion of a new heaven and a new earth is difficult to connect with. It's nearly impossible to visualize and just as difficult to long for. If the world to come conjures up no more than golden streets and celestial shores and chubby angels playing harps, it will remain distant and abstract and depersonalized. But as the opposite of death? As a restoration of what death steals away? That's a promised world we can latch onto. That's a world we can personally long for. But only if we take death personally. Only if we are willing to live with grief.

Grief Clarifies Where Our True Hope Lies

Honesty about death leads to grief, and grief over what's true about this world leads to hopeful longing for the world to come. But there is another way in which our heightened feeling for death's sting clarifies our hope for redemption and resurrection.

---

4. C. S. Lewis, "The Weight of Glory," in *The Weight of Glory and Other Addresses* (1949; New York: Harper, 2001), 30–31, 42. Lewis says that the longing we label "nostalgia" is really "a desire for something that has never actually appeared in our experience." The things from our past that we long for "are good images of what we really desire; but if they are mistaken for the thing itself, they turn into dumb idols, breaking the hearts of their worshippers. For they are not the thing itself; they are only the scent of a flower we have not found, the echo of a tune we have not heard, news from a country we have never yet visited" (30–31).

It helps us see that any hope we have rests completely on a Savior who died and rose again. No other hope will do.

The Heidelberg Catechism opens with a clear and profound question: What is your only comfort in life and in death?[5] I love this question for the assumption underneath it. Any comfort in life must also provide comfort in death. If the object of our hope can't stand up to death's onslaught, it can't offer true hope in life either. There are many things in which we hope throughout our lives. Things we look to for meaning and purpose. Things we accomplish or acquire. Pleasures we enjoy. People we love. We trust these things to deliver. We hope they will endure. And one by one death topples them all.

When you live with honest grief over what death does to life, you recognize that you cannot afford to settle for vague platitudes, for some abstract feel-good hope that things will work out someday. Resurrection as an idea or an aspiration is empty and unsatisfying. For us to know true hope, we need something we can lock onto. We need a living, breathing resurrected *person*. We don't need an ideal. We need a Savior.

I believe this need for a concrete, personal hope in the face of death explains why Jesus orchestrated the Lazarus event the way he did. He knew what his friends needed to see—and that we'd need to see it too.

One of the most striking features of John's story is where he chooses to begin—with an emphasis, over and over, on how much Jesus loves Lazarus and his family. Jesus is doing ministry on the opposite side of the Jordan from Jerusalem when word comes to him that his friend Lazarus is sick. The message is simple but full of meaning: "Lord, he whom you love is ill" (John 11:3). Lazarus's name isn't even mentioned. He is defined by Jesus's love

---

5. See *The Heidelberg Catechism*, 400th anniversary ed. (Philadelphia: United Church Press, 1962), 9.

for him. This love is reaffirmed in verse 5, in case we should miss the point: "Now Jesus loved Martha and her sister and Lazarus" (11:5). Jesus's love for this family is the setup for all that happens next. He loves the man who is dying, and he loves those most deeply affected by his condition.

What would you expect of this miracle worker once he has learned that the one he loves is gravely ill? Don't we expect the loving thing would be to take away the pain right then, right there? When you love someone, as John has insisted Jesus loves this family, isn't the loving thing to protect your beloved from whatever is hurting them?

Nothing in our natural response prepares us for what John tells us next. Putting verse 5 together with verse 6 helps us recognize the stunning conclusion: "Now Jesus loved Martha and her sister and Lazarus. *So,* when he heard that Lazarus was ill, he stayed two days longer in the place where he was."

Precisely because he loved them, he waited. He withheld his power. He did nothing. Why? In the following verses, as Jesus discusses the trip to Bethany with his fearful disciples, he gives the answer, though it's not the answer any of us would expect: "Then Jesus told them plainly, 'Lazarus has died, and for your sake I am glad that I was not there, so that you may believe'" (John 11:14–15).

Jesus is glad that the one he loves has died. He is glad that the ones he loves are in mourning. He is glad he wasn't there to do anything about it. In a way, he's rejoicing in death. It's jarring and, to say the least, unexpected. Why is he glad that this happened? "So that you may believe" (John 11:15). Because he loves them, he allows death to run its awful course. Because he loves them, he wants them to believe. His love for them means not preventing all pain but doing what's best for them. What's best for them, as Jesus defines it, is that they believe. And for them to believe—for them to see Jesus for who he is and cling to him with everything—they need to come face-to-face with death.

When Jesus first meets Martha and Mary on his way to the tomb of their brother, their grief had become a dead end. It was trapped in the past, locked in on what couldn't be changed, fixated on a range of what-ifs. Both greet him with the same charge: "If you had been here, my brother would not have died" (John 11:21, 32). Their grief is trapped in regret. Jesus wants it channeled into hope. He wants them to exchange their "'if only . . .' for an 'if Jesus . . .'"[6]

When Jesus tells Martha that her brother will rise again, she nods in agreement. "I know that he will rise again in the resurrection on the last day" (John 11:24). She "knows" he will rise, but Jesus wants her to *know* it. She has a textbook belief in the future resurrection, but it hasn't penetrated her heart. It hasn't framed her view of this day. She's not looking to the day of resurrection. She's angry that Jesus missed the day of Lazarus's death.

Jesus wants more for her, and for you. He wants us to look to him. "*I am* the resurrection and the life. Whoever believes in me, though he die, yet shall he live, and everyone who lives and believes in me shall never die" (John 11:25–26). "Jesus' concern," D. A. Carson writes, "is to divert Martha's focus from an abstract belief in what takes place on the last day, to a personalized belief in him who alone can provide it."[7] Jesus brought his friends to grief because he wanted them to see *him*. To see that *this* is why we need him so badly. That *this* is what must be made right and fully restored. He wants us to see with the eyes of the heart that we have no other hope in life and in death. And then to look ahead: *if Jesus . . .*

---

6. N. T. Wright, *John for Everyone, Part 2: Chapters 11–21* (Louisville, KY: Westminster John Knox, 2004), 7.

7. D. A. Carson, *The Gospel according to John*, The Pillar New Testament Commentary (Grand Rapids, MI: Eerdmans, 1991), 412.

The Firstfruits from the Dead

Everything depends on Jesus's resurrection. We see that truth only when we've allowed ourselves to see and to grieve over death. When we've recognized our solidarity with Adam in death, we're ready to recognize our solidarity with Jesus in life.

This is the connection at the heart of Paul's great chapter on the resurrection, 1 Corinthians 15: "For as by a man came death, by a man has come also the resurrection of the dead. For as in Adam all die, so also in Christ shall all be made alive" (v. 21).

Paul uses an agricultural image to make his point. He calls Jesus the "firstfruits of those who have fallen asleep" (1 Cor. 15:20). It's a reference to a harvest and how you know it's going to come. You know when the firstfruits rise up from the ground. The arrival of the firstfruits foreshadows and even guarantees the arrival of everything else.

For those of us who don't live from harvest to harvest, perhaps its easier to imagine the coming of spring and its flowers. Where I live the daffodils are the first clear signs. When they start peeking through, sometimes even when there's still snow on the ground, it's a sure sign that there's more to come. Soon enough the daffodils will be followed by green grass, the trees will bud their flowers and then their leaves, the tulips will rise up and then the irises and then the lilies and on and on. The daffodils show the process has begun.

This is how Paul wants us to view Jesus. He wants us to identify ourselves with what happened to him, and to know that what happened to him will happen to us too in time. His resurrection of Lazarus was a powerful sign. But his own resurrection is far more. It is a guarantee. It is the beginning of an organic process that is unstoppable and certain, unfolding in its proper order: "Christ the firstfruits, then at his coming those who belong to Christ" (1 Cor. 15:23).

Think of Paul's image as a gloriously redeemed version of Pascal's nightmare. For Pascal, faced with death, we are each like a condemned prisoner in a line of executed criminals. In every death of every other person we see our own foreshadowed. "Those remaining see their own condition in that of their fellows, and looking at each other with grief and despair await their turn."[8]

But, for Paul, our solidarity with Adam—"as in Adam all die"—only fuels our solidarity with Christ—"so also in Christ shall all be made alive" (1 Cor. 15:22). We look to Jesus as a forecast of our story. We look carefully at what happened to him. We see the victory he won over the grave. And we know that whatever may happen to us on our journey—however great the pain of disappointment, of grief, of death itself—we've been there already in Christ and we're headed where he has already gone. We've set our eyes on Jesus. And, looking at each other with grief and *hope*, we simply await our turn.

---

8. Blaise Pascal, *Pensées*, trans. A. J. Krailsheimer (New York: Penguin, 1966), 165.

General Index

"ache of cosmic specialness," 103
Adam, solidarity with, 183
Adam and Eve, fall of, 71–73, 161
adoption, 76–77, 79–81
affliction, as light and momentary, 151–52
afterlife, 177
animals, 63–65
anxiety, 29, 166–71
appetizer metaphor, 147–48
Aries, Philippe, 43–44, 46n31, 50
ars moriendi (art of dying), 21n4
asceticism, 142
assisted living facilities, 45
attention spans, 91
Augustine, 146, 159

Band of Brothers (HBO series), 168–69
baptism, 80
Barnes, Julian, 21n3, 51–52, 67
Bauckham, Richard, 133, 136
Baxter, Richard, 22n6
Becker, Ernest, 51, 68, 103
Berger, Peter, 104, 110
Bible, 22–23, 56, 68–73
biblical anthropology, 70
biomedicine. *See* modern medicine
Bonhoeffer, Dietrich, 145, 166–67
Bowler, Kate, 53–54
bread of life, 139
brokenness, and presence of Christ, 160
Buddhism, 143
burial clothing, 41
burial plots, 42

Cain and Abel, 161
Camus, Albert, 65–66, 73, 100
Cana, wedding at, 134–37
cancer, 101
cares of the world. *See* problems of life
Carson, D. A., 134n15, 136n19, 181
caskets, 41–42
cemeteries, 19
children of God, 80–83
chronic illnesses, 39
circle of life, 174
Coates, Ta-Nehisi, 32n2
contentment, 158
Corpus Clock (Cambridge), 126
covetousness, 161, 163
credit card metaphor, 128
"culture of abundance," 157

daffodils, 182
death
    on American television, 47–49
    as basic human experience, 19
    conflated with disease, 38, 40
    denial of, 40, 51, 73–74, 174
    denied in funeral customs, 40–43
    detachment from, 19–20, 48
    disorients us, 67–68
    elimination of, 37
    exposes idols, 107
    as final enemy, 55
    as foreign to modern culture, 33–34
    at home, 34, 36
    horrible reality of, 50–52
    as humbling, 62–63, 66, 67
    indignity of, 73

Hambrick-Stowe, Charles, 45n29
happiness
    cultural obsession with, 49–50
    from wealth, 95–96
"happiness effect," 162
health care, access to, 85
heaven, beauty of, 133
hebel, 87n5
Heidelberg Catechism, 179
Hillenbrand, Lauren, 18
historians, 123
homeownership, 85
honesty about death, 150, 154, 158, 172,
    173–74. *See also* death-awareness
hope, 23–24, 26, 168, 171, 178–79
humanity
    difference from animals, 63–65
    dignity of, 69–73
humility, from remembrance of death, 20

identity, 28
    caught up in accomplishments,
        112–13
    transformed by union with Christ,
        75–76
idolatry, 105–6
image of God, 69, 71
immortality, 65
imperishable, 23–24
impermanence, 120–21
infectious disease, 35n8
ingratitude, 163
inheritance, 80–81
inner self, 151
intensive care, 36, 40
irreversibility, of death, 120–21, 127, 130
Isaiah
    on death, 132
    on feast, 132–33

James, William, 86
Jesus Christ
    defeated death, 111, 112, 113
    finished work of, 114
    offers eternal life, 177
    promises of, 23–25, 29
    as the resurrection and the life, 181
    resurrection of, 23, 108, 111, 182–83

    at tomb of Lazarus, 55, 174–75,
        177–81
Johnson, Marcus, 75n18
joy, 27, 29, 141–42, 145–48
justification, 76–79

Kalanithi, Paul, 101–2
Keller, Tim, 74n17, 104n20, 135n17, 149
kenos, 109n23

labor, not in vain, 112, 113–15
Lazarus, raising of, 137, 182
Lewis, C. S., 78, 121, 171–72, 177–78
life, enjoyment of, 26–27
Lints, Richard, 71n14
Lion King (film), 174
loss, 29, 121–27, 131
low expectations, as secret to happiness,
    158

Mather, Cotton, 34–35, 44
memento mori, 22
middle-class life, 93–94
miracles, 134
Mitford, Jessica, 40–43, 54
modern medicine, 35–36
    deception from, 37–40
    and detachment from death, 19
    and extension of life, 53
Moll, Rob, 53
Montaigne, Michel de, 129–30, 132,
    144, 147
Moore, Herman Russell, 12–13
Morris, Leon, 78
mortality, 13, 36
"Myth of Sisyphus" (Camus), 65–66, 73

narcissism, 59, 62, 74
nature, repetitiveness of, 89–90
negative-space portrait, 154
new creation, 75–76
New England Primer, 44–45
new heaven and new earth, 178
new Jerusalem, 178
Nicodemus, 136n19, 137n21
nostalgia, 177–78
Nuland, Sherwin, 33–34, 37, 40
numbering our days, 20–21
nursing homes, 36, 45

Scripture Index

Index page.

THE GOSPEL **COALITION**

The Gospel Coalition is a fellowship of evangelical churches deeply committed to renewing our faith in the gospel of Christ and to reforming our ministry practices to conform fully to the Scriptures. We have committed ourselves to invigorating churches with new hope and compelling joy based on the promises received by grace alone through faith alone in Christ alone.

We desire to champion the gospel with clarity, compassion, courage, and joy—gladly linking hearts with fellow believers across denominational, ethnic, and class lines. We yearn to work with all who, in addition to embracing our confession and theological vision for ministry, seek the lordship of Christ over the whole of life with unabashed hope in the power of the Holy Spirit to transform individuals, communities, and cultures.

Join the cause and visit TGC.org for fresh resources that will equip you to love God with all your heart, soul, mind, and strength, and to love your neighbor as yourself.

TGC.org